PROFIT FROM YOUR VACATION HOME DREAM

THE COMPLETE GUIDE
TO A SAVVY FINANCIAL
AND EMOTIONAL INVESTMENT

CHRISTINE HRIB KARPINSKI

Dearborn™
Trade Publishing
A **Kaplan Professional** Company

This publication is designed to provide accurate and authoritative information in regard to the subject matter covered. It is sold with the understanding that the publisher is not engaged in rendering legal, accounting, or other professional service. If legal advice or other expert assistance is required, the services of a competent professional person should be sought.

President, Dearborn Publishing: Roy Lipner
Vice President and Publisher: Cynthia A. Zigmund
Senior Acquisitions Editor: Mary B. Good
Development Editor: Karen Murphy
Interior Design: Lucy Jenkins
Cover Design: Design Solutions
Typesetting: Elizabeth Pitts

Published by Dearborn Trade Publishing
A Kaplan Professional Company

Printed in the United States of America

05 06 07 10 9 8 7 6 5 4 3 2 1

Library of Congress Cataloging-in-Publication Data

Karpinski, Christine Hrib.
    Profit from your vacation home dream : the complete guide to a savvy financial and emotional investment / Christine Hrib Karpinski.
        p. cm.
    Includes bibliographical references and index.
    ISBN 1-4195-0691-9 (7.25 × 9 pbk.)
    1. Vacation homes—United States—Purchasing. 2. Real estate investment—United States. 3. Vacation rentals—United States—Handbooks, manuals, etc. I. Title.
    HD7289.3.U6K37   2005
    332.63'243—dc22
                                                                              2005008290

Dearborn Trade books are available at special quantity discounts to use for sales promotions, employee premiums, or educational purposes. Please call our Special Sales Department to order or for more information at 800-621-9621, ext. 4444, e-mail trade@dearborn.com, or write to Dearborn Trade Publishing, 30 South Wacker Drive, Suite 2500, Chicago, IL 60606-7481.

DEDICATION

to Zachary with all my love . . .

Contents

PART ONE
FINDING THE PERFECT VACATION INVESTMENT

PART TWO
BUYING THE PERFECT VACATION INVESTMENT

PART THREE
PROFIT STRATEGIES

PART FOUR

ENJOYING YOUR VACATION PROPERTY

I would have to say that writing this second book was much easier than writing my first—not necessarily because it was less work but because of the many people who helped me in the process. That being said, I have many people I want to acknowledge.

For Personal Help and Encouragement

First and foremost to my loving husband and best friend, Tom—thanks for your constant encouragement and loving support. You convinced me to take on this project knowing that it would require personal sacrifices on your part during my absence. Thanks for your selflessness. Tom, I love you more each day.

To my son, Zachary, who dealt with Mom sitting at the computer and talking on the phone many hours every day yet again—you are growing up to be a fine young man and I am proud to be your mom. (But you'll always be my baby, even if you are bigger than me.) Zach, I love you!

To my father, Mihaly Hrib, who through your actions taught me how much hard work and perseverance can achieve—I'm sure you are walking around heaven saying, "See, I did not have the opportunity to go to school, I never learned to read, but my daughter (fer), I made sure she had a good education." Dad, I wish you could have lived to see this book come to fruition. I know you are proud.

To my mom, Judy Hrib Kowalewski, who made me who I am today—no words can explain the impact you have had on me. You are my rock, the stronghold of my foundation. I miss you every day. I am sure you are looking down, smiling at the irony of your little girl who was always in trouble at school for talking too much. Look, Mom. I'm speaking for a living now!

To my in-laws, Ed and Shirley Karpinski—thanks for your love and encouragement. You are wonderful parents to both Tom and me.

To Pappa John Kowalewski, for your love and support—you encouraged me to take the risk to do what I love. Pappa, I'm still having fun!

To my very special aunt, Diana Paradise—thanks for your spiritual guidance and for accompanying me on road trips.

To Hunter Melville, who started as a business contact and became a friend—thanks for reassuring my confidence and assisting me in many ways.

To the Junior Thrashers Pee Wee A hockey team—thanks for keeping Coach Tom and Zach occupied and happy. I don't know if our family could have endured the stress of my writing another book without you! Boy, what a stress reliever it was to cheer (and coach) from the bleachers!

To all my good friends who have always been there for me.

For Professional Help and Encouragement

To my friends, Diane and Kevin Lawton, who learned how to buy and rent their first vacation property—Dede, without your candidness, this book wouldn't include such helpful stories to share with other first-time buyers.

Thanks to all the vacation property owners who have attended my seminars. Thanks also to those of you who took time to answer my survey and share your stories, ideas, and tips.

A warm thank you to Wally Conway for sharing your knowledge and talents through your contributing chapter on home inspections.

Many thanks to all the information contributors listed in the Recommended Resources. And a special thanks to Jack Simpson for the many articles you allowed me to quote.

Thanks to David Hehman for his fabulous Foreword.

Thanks to the Dearborn Trade Publishing people who helped me put this book together. Mary B. Good, many thanks for your persistence in persuading me to become a Dearborn author and for your help with my initial outline.

And a special thanks goes to the one person who helped me shape the words and kept me moving in the right direction, my editor, Barbara McNichol. We jumped through lots of last-minute hoops together, and we did it! Barbara, it was truly my pleasure to work with you.

Most important, I thank the Lord for all the gifts and blessings bestowed upon me.

A friend of mine has been vacationing in Hawaii every year now for five years. He loves it, wants to buy a vacation home there, but just can't seem to get over the hurdles of how to do it. Five minutes into my reading of Christine Karpinski's new book, I knew he HAD to read this book. I wanted to send him my copy immediately.

Profit from Your Vacation Home Dream addresses all the concerns that most people have when they are considering their dreams for vacation, investment, and retirement. More important, the book provides the practical help that people need to make a personal decision. If you are serious about a vacation home for investing and fun and are willing to take the time to learn how to do it and define what you want, this book will lead you to find a great property for great enjoyment—and great investment as well.

As the CEO of EscapeHomes.com, the leading Internet site for second-home buying, I'm in constant contact with second-home buyers. Because the media relies on us for information about the second-home market, EscapeHomes.com studies what consumers need the most and their buying trends. Our second-home surveys have appeared in most major media, including CNBC, MSN, and the *Wall Street Journal.* One compelling point about the current market is the unprecedented number of baby boomers who are coming of age and in search of a second home. We find very strong second-home markets in areas where the climate is mild, and there is easy access to water. However, it is also clear that baby boomers want to protect their investment, either by renting the property out or by selecting an undervalued market.

For baby boomers, the combination of investment, retirement, and vacation all come together in their second-home searching. This particular need is the one addressed so well by Christine's book, and it is done expertly. After all, who wouldn't fall in love with a tropical island house; yet, many could not afford it if there were no way to rent it out due to zoning ordinances or community regulations. Christine helps point buyers to the way to balance both their heart's desire for a beautiful property and the need to keep the practical dollars and cents in mind.

The readers of EscapeHomes.com are well-educated and value accurate and unbiased information to help them make the best buying decision. For several years, we have been happy to have Christine's informative articles on our Web site. Her writing educates our readers on the ways to make money while simultaneously enjoying their vacation homes. Since education is a fundamental value for EscapeHomes.com, we salute Christine for making her knowledge even more accessible through her latest book.

The best thing about this book is the incredible amount of useful materials—from forms to pricing rentals to Web sites. Helping people make an informed decision is clearly Christine's philosophy, and she holds nothing back. Combined with tips on how to locate properties, she guides people step-by-step through the process of second-home research. In our business of helping people find their dream home, we know that the happiest and most successful real estate transactions occur when buyers have educated themselves. When people come to EscapeHomes.com to find a vacation property, we are proud to point them to a book like this.

David Hehman, President, EscapeHomes.com
www.escapehomes.com—the smart source for second homes
E-mail david@escapehomes.com or by phone at 415-252-9500

I never thought I'd actually write a second book after laboring so hard with my first one, *How to Rent Vacation Properties By Owner.* Writing books can be like giving birth to your first child—I'm told that after you've gone through the experience of a first child, you might as well have another so you can apply all you've learned to your secondborn.

Because my husband and I were blessed with only one child, Zachary, my "secondborn" is this book: *Profit from Your Vacation Home Dream: The Complete Guide to a Savvy Financial and Emotional Investment.* I wanted to put to good use the expertise, resources, and experience I've gained since the publication of my first book. I have met and learned from many more people in the vacation property business and have purchased more vacation properties myself.

How to Rent Vacation Properties By Owner was successful because it helped people manage their vacation properties—and perhaps persuaded shy ones to venture out. This book contains even more pertinent information, such as:

- Where to search for vacation properties
- What type of investment property is right for you
- How to find a good real estate agent
- How to finance your second home
- What are good strategies for managing your vacation rental property and the people who help you maintain it

I hope you turn to this book as a primer to help you decipher the nuances of the information you gather and the decisions you're about to make.

BUYING A SECOND HOME

When I first decided I wanted to buy a vacation home, I investigated the Gulf Coast of Florida because it was an area I knew and loved. Remember, my purpose in buying was strictly to have a second getaway home. But from that experience, I started applying what I had learned to the business of being a vacation property investor.

While researching another property for my vacation property investment portfolio, I initially intended to buy additional properties along Florida's Gulf Coast. But in September 2004, I found out that prices in this area had increased dramatically. Unfortunately, rental rates weren't rising enough to keep pace with increased property values. This made it difficult (in some situations, impossible) to realize good cash flow from rental revenue. As a longtime conservative investor, I realized that the more rental properties I purchased, the more conservative my attitude would get. I looked at it this way: The more money I had to spend on an unsure thing, the more money I could lose. And if I lost big, Zachary's college tuition would fly out the window, as would my husband's hopes for early retirement.

So instead of gambling on buying Gulf Coast properties with their rapid inflation factor and risky cash flow, I researched other areas for properties that would meet my criteria for cash flow. Specifically, I looked into the Outer Banks of North Carolina where single-family homes sell for $800,000 and above. Although properties there had also appreciated considerably, rental revenues had kept pace. That meant I could purchase an $800,000 property in the Outer Banks and still realize positive cash flow.

After offering consulting to a client named Caroline, another area—Gatlinburg, Tennessee—caught my attention. Together, we took a three-hour drive from our Atlanta homes and checked out possible vacation homes. In no time, we found three cabins that showed the best rental ratios I've ever seen. We both got so excited that we called our husbands and declared that we wouldn't be back in time to meet the school bus Monday as planned, because we were signing contracts on these cabins (two for me, one for Caroline).

What we learned buying property in Gatlinburg became the backbone for this book.

START FROM WHERE YOU ARE

New investors, take note. It may take a long time to find a property that will generate cash flow immediately, which is especially true for more expensive properties in beachfront communities. I suggest that even if you know what dream property you ultimately want to buy, start with what you can afford today.

An investor I know in a large eastern city owns a brownstone in a historic district. Early on, he knew that when he retired, he wanted to live in the Caribbean. After he got married and had children, his family moved to the suburbs. He turned his brownstone into a long-term rental. Years later, as he came closer to retirement, he converted it into a vacation rental. His plan is to move back into the brownstone once his children leave home. At that time, he'll use the proceeds from the sale of his suburban home to buy his "dream" vacation rental property in the Caribbean. He simply can't afford to buy it yet, but he's taking the right steps toward making it happen.

Similarly, Caroline doesn't view her Gatlinburg cabin as the ultimate retirement property for her husband, Ken, and herself. But Caroline's initial investment of $30,000 (the amount of her down payment) allows them to start building equity and gain experience as vacation homeowners. Over time, they'll be able to "trade up" to their ultimate vacation home, wherever that might be.

YOUR VACATION HOME STRICTLY AN INVESTMENT?

With the dramatic appreciation in many vacation markets, coupled with the dramatic decrease of stock portfolios, a lot of people have turned to buying vacation homes solely as investment opportunities. These people don't intend to take vacations in their homes; rather, they're interested in getting straight returns on their investments.

The process of purchasing a second home strictly as an investment versus as a vacation home requires an entirely different mindset. Investors tend to be money-motivated and have no emotional attachments; vacation homeowners (including those who rent them out) tend to personally use and love their homes.

As I write this in 2005, I can say investing in vacation homes is profitable, but who knows what returns will be at the time you're reading this book. (If you're mainly focused on investing, check in to http://www.escapehomes.com to access information about the hottest markets for vacation investments. This Web site features lists of the top-selling vacation home markets and areas that have the best bargains.)

This book is helpful for investors who want to make money through buying and selling vacation properties. But more so, it's for people wanting a vacation home that will bring them both profit and pleasure.

WILL THE REAL ESTATE BUBBLE BURST?

With today's vacation home appreciation rates at 22 percent annually (see Chapter 10), people often ask me, "Are you worried that the real estate bubble will burst? Prices in this market seem so artificially inflated." I always answer, "No, I don't worry about it because, historically, real estate stands the test of time."

Let me ease your fears about buying a second home during a so-called real estate bubble. You could get soaked in a bubble-burst if you were going into this venture for a quick turnaround. But this book addresses buying property for the long haul. And as long as you can rent out your property and generate revenue from it, experience shows that it will pay for itself.

If property owners in Hawaii had sold their places in the mid-1990s when prices were low, they would have sustained a loss. But those who hung on are now seeing the Hawaiian real estate market bounce back. Remember, investing in real estate is not like day trading; it's more like buying blue-chip stocks. If you're willing to ride out the ups and downs of the market, you'll benefit from the long-term investment you're making.

For example, if I buy a vacation property today for $250,000, and when I go to sell it in 30 years, it's still only worth $250,000—it doesn't really matter to me. Here's why. When I purchase a home, cash flow is always my number one criterion. And if this goal is met, then during the period of ownership, with rental revenues paying all of the expenses, the mortgage is paid off, and it doesn't cost me a dime beyond my initial down payment.

WHAT THIS BOOK DELIVERS

The chapters in this book give you the detailed information you need to take action. You'll learn about balancing the romantic idea of vacation home ownership with realistic facts and experiences. Here's what to expect:

- Chapter 1 provides a list of criteria to help you start envisioning details of your new vacation home.
- Chapter 2 gets you into the nuts and bolts of evaluating your options by type of vacation home.
- Chapter 3 coaches you on how to find a real estate agent who best represents your interests and who can help you get excited about the vacation home community you choose.
- Chapter 4 goes into detail about your financing options and dares to address the biggest obstacles to vacation home ownership—fear of cost overruns and of having no rental activity. It also addresses the pros and cons of investing with family and friends.
- Chapter 5 focuses on aspects of transacting an offer and negotiating a deal from a faraway location. You'll have access to a checklist that will help you make sure nothing gets forgotten.
- Chapter 6 provides details about inspections and insurance coverage. It features contributions from Wally Conway, HGTV's Detective Inspector.
- Chapter 7 delves into how to profitably rent and manage your property as a vacation rental. It addresses pricing, maintenance, booking procedures, and many more how-tos.
- Chapter 8 discusses the question of how to find and work with a management company to manage your vacation property. I'm biased toward self-managing vacation properties, but I understand that it can be a sound choice for some vacation homeowners to hire a management company.
- Chapter 9 explains how you can master advertising for your vacation home.
- Chapter 10 outlines several buy-and-hold strategies to help you increase the value of your vacation property over time.

It also explains how and when to sell your vacation home—sometimes difficult to do because of emotional attachments.

- Chapter 11 offers practical advice on maintenance and home improvements, punctuated by colorful stories of real-life experiences.
- Chapter 12 shows how you can collaborate with your neighbors from afar—a highly beneficial practice that's often overlooked.
- Chapter 13 summarizes key ideas and encourages you to examine the relationship between risk and reward.

Enjoy your journey through these chapters. Even though you're dealing with lots of facts and figures, be good to yourself along the way. And don't lose sight of the romantic ideal of vacation home ownership. After all, that's why you want to get started as a vacation homeowner today.

FINDING THE PERFECT VACATION INVESTMENT

1

WHERE TO BEGIN?

Get ready for this uniquely hybrid venture that combines the romantic idea of owning your own vacation home with that of renting it out to others (the secret to affording that second home). In the process, you'll make decisions based on financial *and* emotional considerations—both in how your vacation home can bring in profits and how you feel about it as a getaway place.

Remember when you bought the home you live in now? Did you make a strictly financial decision? Of course not. In addition to being in the right location, your home needed to have a certain "feel" before you took the plunge and made an offer. Practically, it had to have the right number of bathrooms and bedrooms, as well as details such as a garage, basement, fireplace, kitchen cabinets, the right decor . . . an endless list of things that mattered tremendously. After all, you'd live in this house, play in it, relax in it, and entertain friends in it. Quite possibly you'd raise your children and gather for family holidays in this home, too. The choice you made clearly involved a lot more than finances.

I recommend you adapt that same mindset and enthusiasm when buying a vacation property. But don't get too caught up in finding all the things on your wish list. You may have to make some compromises.

START WITH A PLAN

If you've ever started a business, you know it's wise to start with a business plan. Similarly, think of buying your vacation property as starting a business. If you feel nervous about this process, don't get overwhelmed. No doubt you've created plans for social events at work or at home. What did you do to get started? Perhaps you created a list and wrote down your goals. As you pulled together the details, you added to your list, which evolved into a plan. Now apply the same approach to purchasing your vacation home property. These questions will help you get started:

- Where would you ultimately like to purchase a property?
- How much do homes cost in that location? Are they affordable relative to what you are willing to pay?
- How do you intend to use this property? Primarily as a second home for your own family? Long-term lease? Full-time rental? Vacation rental? Combination of these?
- What are your financial goals for this property?
- What are your expectations for the future of this property?

You get the picture. Add your own questions. You'll find many more questions to add to this list as you keep reading this book. The answers will help you build your plan.

DETERMINING CRITERIA FOR A VACATION HOME

Possibly the most important part of your plan is to determine your criteria before you jump into buying a second home. Though it sounds romantic to say "I own a beach house" or "I'm going to our mountain chalet," I caution you to be realistic about the work that's required. There's more to vacation home ownership than pleasure and profit.

Let's look at the criteria that went into Caroline's plan based on the best location and the right place to buy.

Caroline's Criteria for the Best Location

When determining where to look for a vacation home, Caroline decided the community where she would purchase a vacation home must be

- in a proven area for vacation rentals,
- in a market where property appreciates,
- reasonably close to home, and
- a place family and friends would enjoy.

Proven area for vacation rentals. Caroline wanted to choose an area with long-term viability in the rental market, so it was important to buy in a resort community that's a popular destination for renting vacationers.

Gatlinburg, located in the heart of Great Smoky Mountains National Park, has a high occupancy potential because the park has become an established year-round vacation destination. Attractions within the park include Dollywood, Barbara Mandrell Theater, Ripley's Aquarium of the Smokies, North Carolina Cherokee Casinos, and the towns of Pigeon Forge and Gatlinburg. In addition, the Visitors and Convention bureaus bring in vacationers and conventioneers year-round. In the winter, people from southern climates enjoy the skiing and dustings of snow, and in the summer, the mountains provide a refreshing refuge from the heat. The fall foliage season is breathtaking, and so is the spring-time bloom. Given all these factors, this is a great location to meet Caroline's objective of having vacation property in a strong area for rentals.

Market where property appreciates. Caroline and her husband, Ken, decided to purchase vacation properties as investments for the long run. Buying their first property in Gatlinburg represents their starting point. They don't expect it to build equity rapidly but had confidence that Gatlinburg properties will build over time. Their plan calls for leveraging this property and then investing in more properties to enable them to reach their long-term goal: retiring in their own beachfront home.

Reasonably close to home. Caroline wanted to be in a mountain area fairly close to her Atlanta home so it would be within easy driving distance. Her research told her she could have purchased property in various towns within 45 to 90 minutes of her home. But she learned that Gatlinburg, being three hours from her home in the heart of the Great Smoky Mountains National Park, attracts more than ten million visitors a year. Knowing these vacationers need a place to stay, her chances for successfully renting out her property were excellent. The properties within 90 minutes of her home were not in tourism areas.

Place where family and friends enjoy coming. Caroline and her family had lived in the unchangeable climate of south-central Florida for many years. When they went on vacation, they loved being in different topography and climates found in other states. Besides going on vacations to the seaside, they also enjoyed camping, hiking, and adventuring outdoors. Their desire for outdoor adventures made Gatlinburg a good location for fun family vacations as well as for a profitable rental property.

Caroline's Criteria for the Right Home to Buy

Once Caroline determined which areas suited their needs, she honed in on the criteria for the vacation home itself. The right home had to

- be within her budget of $150,000,
- be fully furnished turnkey ready for rental (most vacation homes are sold that way),
- be convenient to town,
- have a view but not require a steep climb to get to it,
- have at least two bedrooms and two baths, and
- have (or have the space to accommodate) a fireplace, a hot tub, and a pool table.

Why did Caroline choose these criteria? Because from doing her research, she learned that these qualities and amenities were important to potential renters. However, she soon found out she'd have to spend $200,000 to get everything she wanted. In making her final decision, she stuck with her budget but had to compromise on the view, the fireplace, and the pool table.

Meet the budget. For Caroline's family, as for many, finding funds to purchase a second home isn't easy. She's a stay-at-home mom who works part-time, while Ken works in a volatile industry that holds no promise of long-term stability. With a gross income of $70,000 a year and notably excellent credit, their family of four lives on a tight budget. Although "on paper" the bank deemed the couple to be creditworthy, they realized that the amount the bank says it will lend and what they can realistically afford are two different things. They didn't want to feel overextended financially, so they had to make sure their second-home expenses would be covered through rental income.

Other criteria. The Gatlinburg cabin Caroline bought didn't include 100 percent of what they wanted, so compromise became the name of the game. The cabin was fairly close to town, located on a flat piece of land on a third acre but no view. It had two bedrooms and two bathrooms plus a loft, but didn't have a fireplace. Instead of a pool table, she purchased a less-expensive foosball table. Having a fireplace was considered important to renters, and the cost of building one came in within the overall budget.

For Caroline, sticking to her budget may appear to be her number one criterion. But more important to her was the cabin's overall ability to attract renters. This cabin not only came with a proven rental history, but she also knew she could enhance it by adding certain amenities. However, if that weren't possible, she would have walked away or compromised on other criteria like price or location.

The Art of Compromise

A warning is in order here. Politics is often referred to as the art of compromise. Well, the same can be said about real estate, especially when it comes to both the investment and emotional aspects of vacation home ownership. Understand that you should *like* the place before you sign on the dotted line. *Liking* a place isn't the same as *loving* it. Yes, you want to be satisfied with it. You want to be proud of it, feel eager to spend time there, and encourage renters to come. But be realistic and acknowledge that sometimes you just can't get everything you want.

For example, you set your heart on getting a five-bedroom house for your large family. However, while researching the rentals in the communities you selected, you discovered that three-bedroom houses rent more easily than five-bedroom ones. That means it's time for a compromise. Buy the three-bedroom house (your kids might have to share, but they'll survive) to put yourself in a better position for a successful rental. Rule of thumb: Go with the scenario that keeps the cash flowing.

You'll face compromising decisions throughout the buying process, such as whether to buy a beachfront property or one a few blocks away, or whether to buy a condo versus a single-family house. If you're prepared for the tough compromises you'll face, you'll make more intelligent, well-informed choices.

THE CHALLENGES OF OWNERSHIP

The challenges of ownership of a vacation home vary greatly from one individual to another. Do you have children? Do you and your spouse have jobs? Busy people often don't even have the time to mow the lawn at their primary residence, never mind at a second home. Can you afford to hire landscapers and others to maintain your property? What if something goes wrong with a major appliance like the furnace or hot water heater? Will unbudgeted repairs break you?

When it comes down to it, you as the owner will have to spend a minimum of a few weekends a year putting everything in order. Do you have the time, money, and *willingness* to do that? Be honest with yourself about how you want to spend your free time and extra cash before you make any purchase decisions.

I'm sure you've heard the term "sweat equity." Your own hard work plays an important role when it comes to increasing the value of a vacation home that you rent out. Size up every situation carefully before taking action. Know that you can overcome the challenges *if* you have the right information for dealing with them. Even though it involves hard work, remember that owning a vacation home is supposed to be fun.

RECREATIONAL NEEDS

If having an ideal vacation home for friends and family is your number one criterion, pull out old photo albums and reflect on past vacations. Where did you go? What activities did you enjoy? What was your favorite vacation season? Would you want to use your second home year-round? Write down details about the vacations you've taken over the decades. Did you enjoy the mountains, the oceans, or the woods? Did you go to quiet places where you could lie in a hammock and read a book all day, or exciting places with nightlife and fun attractions to visit?

When you purchase a vacation home, you're forced to pick only one of those familiar locations (or similar ones) for the long run. This exercise clues you in to where to start looking for your dream vacation home, so pay close attention as you narrow the choices.

Think about your lifestyle, your hobbies, your likes, and your dislikes. How do you enjoy spending your time recreationally, educationally, and culturally? Which activities are most important to you—skiing, fishing, boating, hiking, tennis, or playing bridge— while on vacation? If being with family is paramount, consider areas where members of your family would like to come and enjoy. In summary, look for locations that reflect who you are and what you like to do.

INVESTMENT COMPONENT

Don't regard buying a vacation home as an extension of a one-shot vacation you took and never visited the area again, even if you enjoyed your time there. It's an entirely different process. You're making a long-term commitment. And because it's your second home, the stakes are higher than if you're buying strictly for the "return on investment." It's not the equivalent of betting your life's savings at the craps table in Vegas. Far from it. Real estate expert Jack Simpson, owner of Holiday Isle Properties, says, "Trying to eliminate risks often creates other risks. Some people put all their money in a 'safe' insured account, only to see their buying power taken away by taxes and inflation. Ask yourself, 'What is the worst that can happen?' To me, the worst thing is seeing your life slip by without risk and reward. That's sad." (See Jack's article on risk and reward in Chapter 13.)

The biggest advantage of investing in real estate is that it almost always appreciates (sometimes quite quickly), and it allows you to buy a property that you couldn't afford otherwise. According to a National Association of Realtors survey conducted in 2002, millions of people know this firsthand. Nearly 6 percent of all homes purchased in the United States in 2001 were second homes. Recent data from the U.S. Bureau of the Census shows a total of 3.6 million seasonal homes in the third quarter of 2002—up from 3.1 million in 1990 and an increase from 1.7 million in 1980. Other census data show there are 9.2 million homes held by owners in addition to their primary residences.

These additional findings also help put the vacation home industry into perspective:

- The typical second-home owner is 61 years old and has a household income of $76,900.
- The vast majority of second-home owners consider their second home to be a good investment.
- The majority of recent second-home buyers who have thought about purchasing a third home report that the recent stock market slump has made them more likely to buy that third property.
- Nearly 78 percent of second homes are vacation homes as opposed to investment homes or land.
- Over half of all second-home owners think of their second home as a family retreat.

- Second-home owners typically live farther from vacation homes than from investment homes.
- Most vacation home owners never rent the home; most investment home owners never use their homes.
- Fifteen percent of second-home owners cited income as a factor for buying or keeping their second home; 16 percent responded that they wanted to "diversify investments."
- One in six second-home owners over 55 plans to make their second home their primary residence after retirement.

If you buy smart, you can build up a good deal of equity in just a few years (see Chapter 10). Yes, at first you may have to rent out your property for most of the year just to break even. And it probably won't be a cash cow, so don't set your expectations too high. But be patient. As your equity builds and rental fees increase over the years, you can rent it less often and still stay ahead financially. Know that your property will eventually become profitable. In the meantime, you have a wonderful place to spend your future vacations—with no reservations required.

MARKET CONSIDERATIONS

When you're looking for a destination, don't throw a dart at the map and take your chances. Instead, ask lots of questions. What is the rental history of the property you might purchase? What is the competition like for rentals in that area? Is it already glutted with vacation homes? How long is the busy season? It's critical to ask—and evaluate—everything before you make a decision. Keep this credo in mind as you begin this new adventure: Be an actively involved owner! Gather all of your facts. Know exactly what you're buying, what properties compete with yours, and who your potential renters will be. Do this background work thoroughly and you'll soon enjoy a vacation home that pays for itself—one that will turn a profit for you over time.

When considering the best location for your second home, don't jump to an overly simplistic conclusion, such as "Well, I live in Minnesota and hate the snowy, freezing-cold winters, so I'll buy a vacation home in sunny Florida where we can escape every winter. That'll be the life!"

Well, maybe. Then again, maybe not. Have you thought that plan through completely? The distance between Minnesota and Florida makes it difficult to travel to your vacation home easily by car. That means every time you need to visit your property, you'll have to fly, which may not be convenient or cheap. You'd have to deal with tedious layovers and connections, plus post–9/11 security measures and long waits. The result? Chances are you'll feel exhausted before you even arrive at your home away from home. I'm not exaggerating about this; it's a critical factor.

While having a vacation home in an exotic locale far from home might have its appeal, it's often not practical. Now you have more questions to add to your list. How often will you visit your second home? What is the ideal travel distance by car or plane? I suggest searching for places within a three- to six-hour drive from where you live. For a vacation home you'd use primarily on weekends, I suggest looking for a property within 300 miles from home. That seems to be the farthest most people will travel for weekend getaways, particularly when their leisure time is limited.

MORE BENEFITS OF SECOND-HOME OWNERSHIP

When selecting criteria for your vacation home purchase, consider situations in which your property could serve other purposes. What if you have a major problem with your primary home—for example, the furnace goes out or the basement floods in a bad storm? What if you (or your spouse) lose your job in today's hard-to-predict economic environment and need to sell your primary home?

In 2004, thousands of Floridians had to evacuate their homes in the face of four hurricanes. Those who own vacation properties felt relieved that they had a place to go—and so will you if disaster strikes your primary home.

In the United Kingdom, the employers' retirement accounts are not backed by the government as they are in the United States. During the economic boom of the 1990s, a large number of employers made risky investments, which resulted in employees having to retire without a pension. Many of these employees were forced to sell their primary residences to cover daily living expenses. Fortunately, those who already owned vacation or investment homes had a choice; they could sell either their primary home or their second home to keep going. If you faced this dilemma, wouldn't you like to have that choice, too?

This example shows why I recommend that you approach buying your second home in the same way you'd purchase a primary residence. After all, you're still purchasing a living experience—a place where you'll go for much-needed relaxation throughout the year and perhaps during the rest of your life.

2

TYPES OF VACATION
HOMES TO CONSIDER

You always have a choice of buying an existing property or buying into a new development in your targeted community. Your options include everything from high-maintenance homes to fixer-uppers to condominiums and more. Let's examine various options for your vacation home purchase.

HIGH-MAINTENANCE HOMES

"It's a great house. Yes, it's old but perfect . . ." Have you heard those words before, or maybe even said them?

Let me just say as a previous owner of a 100-year-old house, these two words never go together: *old and perfect*. Older homes require a lot of unseen maintenance. That being said, you might be wise to pass on a property that requires a lot of maintenance. Even if you are the handyman type, you'll find this venture to be different than simply fixing up things around your own residence.

It won't be as simple as a quick trip to the local home improvement store to pick up a new storm door or a washer for a leaky kitchen faucet. Know that a high-maintenance house will require your frequent attention in both time and money. And here's the real drag: You'll have to accomplish it *from a distance.* You'll quickly find out that every time your vacation home needs maintenance, you'll face a substantial effort.

Hiring workers to do the job, as I'm sure you realize, can be quite expensive. You're also at a disadvantage because you're not on-site supervising their work to make sure they don't run up bills unnecessarily. There's truth in the old adage "If you want something done right, do it yourself." But that can be difficult when you live hundreds of miles away.

Therefore, my advice is to buy a low-maintenance property rather than one requiring constant maintenance. I know that solution sounds incredibly simple, but you might be surprised how obvious things can be overlooked.

How do you find out the condition of a house? Make sure you hire an expert to inspect your home. (See Chapter 6 for more details.) *Taking this step is always money well spent.* When reviewing the home inspector's report, pay particular attention to the condition of the major aspects of the home: the foundation, the structure, roofing, plumbing, electrical wiring, and the heating and air-conditioning systems—all noncosmetic items with functions that aren't apparent to the naked eye. Repairing them can be expensive and time consuming. If you buy a home without problems in these areas, you'll save yourself lots of headaches and dollars in the years to come.

FIXER-UPPERS

Now, many people think it's a bargain to do the exact opposite of buying a maintenance-free house. They intentionally buy one with many problems because it can be purchased at a bargain price. They rehab their "diamond in the rough" and end up with a more lavish home for a lower-than-market price.

While this approach may sound good in theory—and millions of homeowners make money this way—doing a successful rehab can be challenging. Did you ever see the movie *The Money Pit?* This exaggerated Hollywood comedy contains a valuable message: Rehabbing can eat all your money. When you add up the final rehab numbers, inevitably the project comes in overbudget. Don't forget, during the period of making repairs, you can't rent out your property, so you have to put your incoming cash flow "on hold" longer than you may have planned.

I certainly don't think you should rule out the idea of buying a fixer-upper completely, but carefully consider potential problems before moving forward.

Lydia and her husband purchased a duplex that was a fixer-upper. The downstairs unit came with a signed seasonal lease from June to October, 2004, at a rental price of $10,500, or $2,100 a month. Lydia said, "Having it already rented both hurt and helped us. It helped us because we didn't have the time to fix up both units at once, and we didn't have to worry about renting this circa-1970 apartment complete with harvest gold kitchen appliances, rust-colored carpet, and linoleum tiles in disrepair during that time. But having it rented hurt us because we received a lot less money than we could get on our own with weekly rentals. All told, it was probably a wash financially."

Once they completely renovated the upstairs unit, they had a phenomenal rental season, despite the fact that they'd listed the units with three Realtors and not one lead came from them. Said Lydia, "We got rentals on our own through a few rent-by-owner Web sites. I realized we had weak photos on our listing, but we can improve them during the off-season."

COSMETIC UPGRADES

Many people overlook purchasing properties that just need a measure of TLC—tender loving care. Those who can see past the blemishes and visualize a polished result—and willingly add their own sweat equity—are able to pay less money and realize quick appreciation.

Before Caroline bought her furnished Gatlinburg cabin, it was sparsely decorated and didn't have a fireplace, but she saw that with a bit of imagination and decorating—plus the addition of a fireplace—it could be a charming place. In addition to a new fireplace, simply by purchasing some throw pillows, hanging pictures on the wall, putting centerpieces on the tables, and adding other touches, she gave the cabin a personality and increased its rental value, too.

While Caroline compromised in the purchasing stage, the following owner actually looked for as-is property that needed cosmetic upgrades.

Already owning and successfully renting an investment property, Erin was ready to purchase another. She could see possibilities of beauty among the scruffiest properties and shopped for properties selling for less than market value. One she found was $20,000 less than comparable properties. But you guessed it—it was ugly. It had outdated 1970s decor, little curb appeal, and the need for some TLC. But she went for it. She and her husband worked for two solid weeks painting, pulling up carpeting, installing hardwood floors, extending decks and installing a hot tub, renewing the landscaping, tossing old furnishings, and adding new ones. They spent $12,000 plus their two weeks of hard work and had a diamond to show for it.

PRECONSTRUCTION HOMES

Why not buy a preconstruction vacation home? Many people do. But before you proceed, think carefully about a whole set of factors.

First, realize that in most cases, buying preconstruction can be more expensive up front than buying an existing home because you usually have to come up with a larger down payment and, once it's built, purchase all of the furnishings. Builders sell preconstruction homes at a reduced price, so they can bring in money and get the project off the ground. That works to the buyers' benefit in the form of accelerated appreciation in the years immediately following a purchase.

Buying a preconstruction property can be expensive initially, but investors are often better off in the long run because of the appreciation factor. (See Chapter 10 for a discussion on buying and holding properties.) In all likelihood, you will see better appreciation in your first few years of ownership with a preconstruction than with preowned homes.

Here's how Jack Simpson explained the process of buying a preconstruction home:

> "First, the developer acquires the land and applies for a construction loan. To reduce financial risks, lenders typically require the developer to sell at least half of the condo units with a binding contract before funding the construction loan. Since it is harder to sell sky and paper than something you can actually see and feel, the developer discounts the purchase price to achieve the required presales. Presales are usually done first on a nonbinding reservation agreement with a few thousand dollars as a good faith deposit. This is called the reservation stage. Buyers can opt out anytime in this stage and receive a full refund.

"After the lender-required units are reserved, the developer delivers the final condominium documents to the buyers. These documents describe the condominium project in great detail. This is called the contract stage. Buyers then have 15 days to look over the documents and decide whether to go hard on the contract or to back out and have their reservation deposit refunded. Going hard on the contract normally requires buyers to make an additional deposit, which, combined with the reservation fee, will be 20 percent of the purchase price. At hard contract stage, the deposit then becomes nonrefundable. Some fallout may occur as the result of a few buyers opting out. With the required number of firm contracts in hand, the developer has the construction loan funded and building begins. Buyers do not close and start making payments until the project is completed with a certificate of occupancy."

Purchasing preconstruction property is similar to buying an initial offering for stocks: you're taking a gamble that the value will increase.

I have been particularly successful in purchasing preconstruction. I bought a condominium in Panama City, Florida, in December 2002 for $212,000. I put 10 percent down, which was $21,200. Today, that property is worth $575,000 and the complex is still not completely built. Just as stock prices can go up and down, so can the price that a property is worth. I'm confident that I will always be able to sell it for more money than I purchased it for. Purchasing preconstruction is all about being in the right place at the right time.

CONDOMINIUMS

If you decide to buy a condominium for your vacation home, realize that there will almost certainly be a condo fee, which is assessed monthly, quarterly, or biannually. This fee helps fund the operations of the association. A board of officers is elected by the owners to oversee these operations (either directly or through a property manager).

Don't let paying the association fee scare you away and cause you to overlook the many benefits of purchasing a condo. For starters, owning a condo means easier maintenance than owning a house. After all, there is no roof to repair, no lawn to mow, no snow to shovel, and no leaves to rake. Moreover, a condominium complex likely includes common amenities you won't find in a single-family dwelling. These amenities, such as Olympic-size pools, hot tubs, golf courses, health clubs, and more, can go a long way to attracting quality renters.

And here's another big advantage: Because developers know all the ideal spots to purchase real estate and have the deep pockets to acquire it, condos get built in an area's best locations—right on the beach, next to that big ski mountain, or closest to the main tourist attraction in the area. Developers get their hands on the most coveted land and turn it into a beautiful destination development. What's more, it usually comes with great views, which vacationers desire. As Jack says, "Always consider the view value of a property before buying. Properties with a good view will rent better and be worth more when it's time to sell."

On the downside, condo association rules could limit the use of your property as a rental. For example, you may be required to occupy the premises yourself for a certain number of weeks each year or deal with age restrictions and quiet times, which may not be to your liking. This may mean that you can't rent it for as many weeks as you may want.

Here's another disadvantage: Sometimes you are charged "special assessments" for improvements to common areas that you'd never have to pay on a single-family home.

Still, looking at the big picture, consider the possibility that the benefits of condo ownership outweigh the drawbacks. Do your homework!

TIME-SHARES—BE CAUTIOUS

When I talk about buying vacation property, some people immediately assume I mean time-shares. That's not what I'm referring to. In fact, I see few benefits and many disadvantages to buying time-shares as investments. When you buy a vacation property, you own it 52 weeks of the year; when you buy a time-share, you only "own" it one week of the year. Is that true ownership, especially when you consider its resale value?

Let's say you buy a time-share for a week and it costs $20,000. What's the real cost if you bought at that rate for the whole year? Do the math: 52 weeks × $20,000 = approximately $1 million. Take a fresh look at the property and ask, "Is it really worth $1 million?" I'm willing to bet it's not. Its value is probably closer to a similar property down the street priced at $200,000 or $300,000. Why do people get involved with the time-share concept in the first place? It's usually because of high-pressure sales tactics, which should be a sign from the start that it's a bad idea for the buyer.

3

FINDING A REAL
ESTATE PROFESSIONAL

When purchasing vacation homes, it's a given that you need to know a lot about the area in which you want to buy. You also need to know about strict governing rules, regulations, and laws that apply exclusively to vacation rental homes. For example, many times homes in resort communities are difficult to insure properly, and some local laws even restrict an owner's ability to rent. You need to know about these!

The best way to overcome any obstacles is to find an excellent real estate agent who's experienced in vacation homes in your targeted communities. Both in the initial search and when transacting a deal, you'll rely heavily on the knowledge of your agent. Keep these questions in mind when choosing an agent:

- Can that person provide statistics and concrete information about the community?
- Does he or she fully understand the local laws and regulations?

- Is he or she willing to go the extra mile to make the closing go smoothly?

If you don't work with a qualified agent, you could lose out on benefiting from the expertise that person brings to the table. That's especially true if your vacation home is in a state that's unfamiliar to you. Do thorough research and make sure you pick a real estate agent who fits your needs—*plus* find one you enjoy spending time with.

QUALITIES YOU WANT IN YOUR AGENT

As vacation home owner Ed Reese said about real estate agents:

"Yes, there are absolutely Johnny-come-latelies who are lazy and looking to make the easy buck in real estate, and there are also professional, hardworking, loyal agents. I've had both. The salespeople from the last agency I worked with had an ambitious sales and marketing machine that provided every statistic I could ever have wanted. This firm also has agents who are strictly 'buying agents' or 'selling agents' because different skill sets are needed for the two.

"I absolutely want a volume-oriented, marketing-whiz, deal-closer selling my house. However, I don't really want the same type of person helping me buy a home. I would want a buyer's agent who focuses on research and responsiveness, who can be pleasant for hours on end and has experience in housing trends. The real estate agent is an important key to success in our industry. Good ones are worth finding."

Some people feel obligated to deal with the first agent they contact, but don't fall into that trap and let that determine your choice. Like this owner said, you'll spend a lot of time with the agent you choose, so make sure you feel comfortable and can trust that person's expertise.

Memberships and Specialized Training

When checking an agent's credentials, determine his or her education and training as well as affiliations with state and national trade associations. Trade participation, training, and industry credentials don't guarantee an agent's expertise, but they do indicate a professional commitment that portends better service for you. Plus, those with trade group memberships have an advantage because they are privy to listings, market information, and other data that nonmembers may have difficulty obtaining.

In addition, you can look for agents who have completed specialized training in vacation home sales. Agents can now take classes and earn an RRS designation. RRS stands for Resort Recreation Specialist, and obtaining this certification is based on a curriculum developed by Gee Dunsten and Leroy Houser. (See http://www.resortrecreation.com for full details on qualifications and classes offered as well as a list of agents who have completed the certification training.) They expect to have 4,000 people certified through the program by the end of 2005.

Both Gee and Leroy are qualified instructors for the Council of Residential Specialists (CRS) designation for real estate agents. Gee stated, "National Association of Realtors statistics show that 20 percent of the agents are doing 80 percent of the work and that ratio has probably shrunk even more to 10/90." That's why it's wise to look for agents with specialized training in the resort areas. You want to find that 10 percent who are doing almost all that work. They're truly the experts!

Expressing Thanks

It may sound trivial, but I consider agents' gift-giving practices a crucial measuring stick of how they value their clients. Gestures of appreciation, such as giving a dinner certificate or a housewarming gift at closing, show they value their clients' business. In a seller's market, agents don't have to work extremely hard for their sales, but I think it's still critical for them to build rapport and express gratitude. So ask everyone you talk with if an agent cared enough to show appreciation after the sale closed. If the answer is yes, that's a sign of professionalism and can be another reason to work with that person.

RESORT AGENTS

Buyers want an agent who specializes in exactly what they're looking for and who willingly takes the time to define what that is. Some agencies double as property managers; some specialize only in buying properties; and others only in selling. Decide what you want early on. Overall, though, you want a local real estate advocate with whom you can build a trusting, long-term relationship—someone who becomes your "friend at the beach" or wherever you're looking to buy.

As a buyer, please realize that real estate agents in small towns don't tend to be aggressive, especially compared to those working in big, bustling cities. Often, small-town agents aren't willing to accommodate people looking at properties if the timing conflicts with other happenings in their lives. Said Gee Dunsten, who trains experienced agents in the specialty of selling vacation homes: "Part of the attraction of being an agent in a resort community is having a laidback lifestyle. Often, they work very hard in the high season so they can kick back in the low season."

When comparing the process of buying a primary home versus a vacation home, the dynamic differs greatly. Job transfers and other factors can add pressure to the process of selecting a primary home. Buyers can be anxious to relocate quickly. But if you bring an aggressive big-city attitude to the task of buying a vacation home, you may encounter resistance. After all, agents live in resort communities because they love the slow pace compared with cities and suburban areas. So don't rock the boat. Just slow down and get to know the area well.

Patience is a good quality for agents to have, considering most vacation home buyers take their time to shop. They investigate several communities and compare dozens of variables against one another. On average, purchasing a vacation property takes 18 to 30 months from start to finish—a process that requires persistence as well as patience. Good agents will facilitate opportunities for their buying clients to visit properties on weekends and will remain available to communicate. They'll also be available to interpret information and follow up on requests as well as smooth the way for a seamless transaction.

Questions to Ask

If you know friends or vacation home owners who've recently bought properties in your target community, ask if their agents were reliable, professional, and trustworthy. Get names of these agents and interview several. In your quest for the perfect match, here are questions to ask when interviewing prospective agents:

- How long have you been selling?
- Do you own properties yourself in this community?
- Are you a good negotiator? Ask for examples of specific deals that they've negotiated.

- What areas of town do you specialize in? (Note that buying property in specific parts of an area can differ significantly, as will the expertise of the agents in those specific areas. For example, a home on the golf course comes with different concerns than buying on the beach in terms of insurance and other factors.)
- What resources do you have that would support my purchase? What resources does your office provide?
- Would I be dealing exclusively with you or with someone else?
- If someone else, how will that person benefit the transaction?
- Who will facilitate the execution of the contract?
- Who facilitates the transaction in the background?
- Who actually talks to the seller's agent?

In my experience, it's critical to be up front and honest with the agents you work with. I encourage you to eagerly share your list of criteria with them, so you don't waste time on properties that don't meet your criteria.

Questions Agents May Ask You

Agents will have a list of questions to ask prospective clients like you. Anticipate how you'd answer these questions:

- What specific criteria are you looking for? Which ones do you rank highest?
- Have you owned vacation property before? Do you own some now? (This helps agents learn the level of knowledge you have as a buyer.)
- What other communities are you looking in?
- Can I refer you to a colleague in those areas?

- What are your goals for this property?
- Will you be renting it out? If so, do you need referrals to a rental agent or a property management company?

Dual Agency

I strongly urge you to avoid stepping into a "dual agency" situation. Dual agency means that your buying agent is the same person who has listed the home. I feel that anyone wearing both hats simply *cannot* remain unbiased in the transaction. For your own best interest, just say from the start you won't buy from the listing agent. Period. Then immediately ask for a referral to a different agent and continue your search.

WHERE TO FIND AGENTS IN RESORT COMMUNITIES

Ultimately, when looking for an agent, you'll want to source those who are qualified to sell resort properties—ideally those who have earned their RRS certification. But in reality, there may not be RRS-certified agents in your target area. What do you do?

Talk to Locals

Find out which agents the local people think are good. Go to restaurants and local hangouts. Think back to the *Andy Griffith Show* and the Mayberry small-town culture of many resort communities. Where did the townsfolk get their gossip and good tips? From barbers and hairstylists, of course. I suggest you wait until you visit that community to have your hair cut. Make an appointment at the local barbershop and ask questions while getting a haircut. Barbers tend to know the professionals who are well respected in their communities!

Agent Meredith McKenzie gave this piece of advice: "I have found that a good practice is to hang out in the local coffee shops (the ones with GOOD coffee) and talk to local outfitters (e.g., ski operators, sport fishing companies, whitewater rafting/kayaking outfits). Because outfitters have clients they want repeat business from, they are more apt to recommend agents who are professional and know their stuff."

Also contact vacation home owners in the community and ask them which agents they'd recommend. To locate these homeowners, identify properties similar to the one you'd like to purchase in the areas of consideration through their Internet listings. (See Web sites listed in Appendix B.)

Another idea is to attend a local charity event or get involved in a community service. Volunteer for an event on a weekend when you're visiting and talk to other volunteers about living in that community. They'll likely be delighted to give you a flavor for the area and the people living there.

You may be thinking that all these things add up to a lot of effort just to find a real estate agent. Remember, you're not just looking for an agent—you're looking for a home. All in all, they're fabulous ways to feel like a member of your new—if only part-time—community. There's a special feeling you get when you go to your second-home community, walk into a restaurant or store, and have people greet you by name. That's what makes it a home.

Agents Everywhere

Local real estate markets are booming across the country. In his article "How to Choose a Real Estate Agent" (*RealtyTimes,* December 10, 2004), noted real estate journalist Broderick Perkins wrote: "Nationwide, the number of licensed real estate agents has swollen to 2.5 million, according to the Association of Real Estate Law Officials and National Association of Realtors (NAR). The

NAR says membership has risen 25 percent over the past five years to more than 1 million." Given that, how can you sift through a large number of available agents to find the best one for you?

The article offered tips such as these: Never hire an agent you meet by chance at an open house, through the Yellow Pages, or on the Internet without fully checking that person's credentials, experience, and practices. Get several recommendations from friends, family members, coworkers, and others who have recently worked with a competent agent. Ask each referred agent to recommend one or two top-notch agents who could fulfill your needs. Also ask to talk to past clients, both buyers and sellers. He wrote: "Ask for numbers of homes the agent found for buyers and sold for sellers over comparative periods. Don't accept a dollar amount answer. Ask for the addresses of recent transactions. Scan the list for homes similar in price to what you can afford. Determine if the homes are in the general neighborhood or community where you are buying. If so, get the agent to talk about what you can expect for your money and the pros and cons of the neighborhood or community."

Finding an agent who listens well is also important. Perkins wrote: "As you ask questions and discuss your needs, consider how well the agent listens to your anxieties, fears, and concerns. You want to feel that the agent cares more about your needs than collecting the commission or making a quota."

I wish I had done more homework to find an agent when purchasing my two cabins in Gatlinburg, Tennessee. First, I went to the Internet, which is a good starting point for finding a real estate agent in a particular area. This search has helped me and many other investors find above-average agents who specialize in resort areas.

This time, the agent I found from the Internet was aggressive in landing my business. But I soon found out he wasn't as knowledgeable as I wanted. I hate to admit this, but because of my experience buying vacation homes, I got cocky and decided I didn't need a high level of ser-

vice from an agent. I thought I'd be okay working with this one–the first one I spoke with.

Did he show me properties? Yes. Did he facilitate the transaction as smoothly as I needed? No. That's where his inexperience cost me a lot of time and money compared with other more qualified agents I've worked with.

As an example, after I walked through one of the cabins I wanted to buy, I asked him to cite the broken railing on the deck on the offer contract. He said it wasn't necessary to put that detail in the contract, that it would get noted at the home inspection stage. However, the in-spector's initial report didn't include the broken railing. That omission cost me time in phone calls convincing the inspector to come out again at no charge to have another look. In the end, repairing the hand rail-ing became an outstanding issue at the closing table. We had to put money in escrow to deal with the after-closing repairs.

I learned about another critical issue that got overlooked by the real estate agent less than a week before closing–an easement issue that af-fected parking rights. In my opinion, a good real estate agent should have told me about that from the beginning and understood the situa-tion before it ever became an issue.

To top it off, because my agent knew he wouldn't get paid that day, which was scheduled at 4 PM on a Friday, he showed up late for clos-ing. I was dumbfounded. Is getting paid the only reason he came to the closing?

Given this situation, I got upset with myself for not doing the kind of due diligence that I teach others to do! My advice? Beware that the more complacent you get, the sloppier you'll become about the details of purchasing real estate. Don't get caught up in the moment so much that you don't source and screen good real estate agents.

Search the Internet

You can find names of agents by doing a search on Google or Yahoo! by putting in the name of the community plus "realtor" plus "vacation home." Then check out selected agents through their Web sites. In today's market, I've found there's a direct correlation between great agents and high-quality Web sites. Escape Homes.com is one of my favorite Web sites for sourcing good agents.

As you do your detective work, here's what to look for on the agents' Web sites:

- Do they have information about how to rent a house or condo?
- Are statistics about rental revenues of their clients included? Are they marketing their listings as rentals or as second homes?
- Do they include information such as taxes, HOA dues, and information about accessibility?
- Do they have high-quality photographs on their listings?
- How much community information is included besides links to other sites? (Agents committed to helping buyers spend time and money to put up an information-rich Web site that caters to their clients and prospective clients.)
- Do they include recommended restaurants and local attractions?

In general, look for a wealth of specialized information on the agents' sites. After all, if they can't tell their prospective clients where to get fresh ahi tuna in a community where fresh fish is a big attraction, how can they know about the best real estate available? You can expect that the agent who takes time to post good answers to common questions will spend quality time with you finding the right vacation home.

Here's the umpteenth reason I shouldn't have used the agent I did in Gatlinburg. He didn't have a good Web site. And one more reason—when we asked about good places to eat for lunch, he couldn't even recommend one!

"THE REAL ESTATE AGENT DOESN'T TAKE ME SERIOUSLY"

This scenario commonly happens in a popular resort town: A couple comes to town and, on a whim, decides to spend a day looking at properties there. Possibly their dream home of the future is right in this vacation mecca! But the first few agents they approach barely give them the time of day. Why? The agents aren't willing to supply vital information because they don't regard the couple as serious buyers. Perhaps they assume they are buyers who can't afford a second home. More likely, they assume this request to see property is a diversion and not a sincere effort to buy a vacation property.

Meredith McKenzie, an agent in Ventura, California, sells properties near the ocean as well as vacation homes in the Sierra Nevada mountains. She said that serious buyers visit the area often and love it. She considers those who live within three or four hours from the resort area most likely to be serious buyers. They show interest in forming an ongoing relationship with a good agent because they see the value of that person's service in making their dream home idea come to life.

Remember, just as a buyer looks for a good match, so does the agent.

Signing a Buyer's Agreement

In Meredith's opinion, most buyers fail to recognize what an exclusive buyer/seller agreement can do for them. Simply stated, an exclusive buyer's agreement means that the real estate agent can't show anyone else a property until you (the buying client) say you're not interested in it. For the real estate agent, that agreement differentiates buyers from lookers and adds a fiduciary responsibility to the relationship.

Not all agents agree that having a buyer's agreement is necessary. Gee, who has completed close to 3,000 transactions, has never had people sign a buyer's agreement because "I believe I have to earn that exclusive relationship with the service I provide." Whether you choose to sign a buyer's agreement up front is, of course, up to you and depends on your comfort level with your agent.

I personally choose not to sign a buyer's agreement when I'm looking at properties, but once I've found a property I want to buy and I'm ready to make an offer, then I sign a buyer's agreement. At that time, I'm prepared to commit to this agent. Indeed, I need this agent to commit to me and only me. In my eyes, a buyer's agreement provides both moral and fiduciary exclusivity between my agent and me.

FOR SALE BY OWNER

If you find a property for sale by owner, known as a FSBO (pronounced "fizzbo"), you could save money and enjoy doing the transaction, or you could experience a nightmare. Most commonly, buyers walk into situations they simply aren't informed about. What if some special assessments are coming up and the seller doesn't disclose that? For example, one investor bought a property for a rental but didn't know the city had recently rezoned the area, cutting out the rental market. Working with a real estate agent can help you find out details about what's going on locally.

> I *considered buying a FSBO property in Florida; I live in Georgia; the property owner lived in Tennessee. I could see that facilitating that transaction could have been one headache after another. Even though some regard having an agent as an expense, I look at the agent I choose as an expert–someone who really knows the business. In this case, when I decided to buy this FSBO, I went to a real estate agent and asked him to facilitate my sales transaction for a flat fee. (A reasonable amount to pay is 1 or 2 percent of the sales price.)*

HOW GOOD AGENTS COVER YOUR INTERESTS

When I initially looked at one building in a vacation area, its price was considerably less than others in the same category. Through the agent, I found out that this building had been hit twice by hurricanes. If another hurricane came along, it would be considered uninsurable. For that reason, I walked away.

Agents are well versed in local building and zoning codes; insurance issues regarding erosion, hurricanes, and floods; and land issues. They also can help you determine certain property rights. I considered buying a lakefront building until I learned it was on Corps of Engineers land, which is protected. I didn't want to tangle with federal laws, so I let this one go, too. Your agent can provide a valuable service by sourcing crucial information that will prevent legal entanglements down the road.

BUYING THE PERFECT VACATION INVESTMENT

4

REVIEWING YOUR FINANCING OPTIONS

A lot of people don't own a second home because they fear they can't afford one. After writing monthly checks for their mortgage, car payments, and household and child expenses, they don't have much money to spare.

But you picked up this book because it tells you that you don't have to be rich to own a second home. Indeed, few rich people rarely start out that way. You have to spend money to make money. I believe there's an important relationship between risk and reward—a philosophy that is articulated well in an article by Jack Simpson in Chapter 13.

For me, buying vacation properties has been among the safest investment choices I've ever made. I can sleep at night knowing that I can both manage this investment strategy and not dip into my family budget. For you, I hope that acquiring money becomes secondary in your decision to invest in a second home for pleasure and profit. In today's financial climate of low interest rates, it's become easy to borrow money. The question to ask yourself is this: Is investing in a vacation home a business you want to get into and learn to run effectively? If your answer is yes, then having the money on hand to do this becomes secondary. Where there's a will there's a way.

Think about how some restaurants got started. Someone's Uncle John took the risk to open a restaurant because everyone told him how fabulous his cooking was. First, he had to decide to start this business, and then follow up by finding the financing to do it.

The same can be said about investing in a vacation property as a business. You're motivated to make this work. Of course, you may wonder whether renters will come, just like Uncle John wondered if customers would come to his restaurant. But with a clear vision and smart marketing, you can realize the message of the movie *Field of Dreams*—"If you build it, they will come." After all the years I've owned vacation rentals, even I get butterflies wondering if "they will come." But once the renters start calling, the butterflies go away.

> **W**hen she first thought about investing in a second home, Caroline couldn't "see" that renters would actually come to her rental property. If no renters would come, how could her family afford to buy a vacation home? But while visiting Gatlinburg and researching properties there, she noticed (feeling both annoyed and encouraged) how the roads were jam-packed with traffic. Then a lightbulb went off. These drivers jamming the roads were all vacationers—all potential renters—and she "saw" the possibilities. She reasoned that all these people vacationing needed some place to stay—so why not hers. At that point, she realized that if she "built" it (and advertised it, of course), they would come!

BUY WHAT YOU CAN AFFORD

You can always start small and, through leveraging, work yourself up to that "ultimate" property. (You'll learn more about leveraging in Chapter 10.) I know you're probably saying, "By the time I can afford it, that 'ultimate' property will cost a lot more." Yes, that's true, but your other investments should have appreciated at the same rate.

If you're like many people, shopping and especially bargain hunting are a way of life. So why does your consumer savvy disappear when it comes to financing a home? Just mention the word *mortgage* and doubt descends like a huge dark cloud.

Examine how you honestly feel about home financing. I once saw an ad for a mortgage company showing a "survey" that stated the top three things people hate to do. The number one item on the list was to go through the mortgage process, and number two was to have a root canal. I have to admit, mortgaging is the part of the purchasing process that I dislike the most! I think it's because it's difficult to really understand the process. Let me help cut through any confusion you might have.

BE A SAVVY MORTGAGE CONSUMER

When you purchased a car, perhaps all the salesperson's double-talk gave you the impression that you're not just getting a retail price for your trade-in but you're getting a *great* retail price. Wrong. At best, you are getting a wholesale price. And beyond the trade-in, you have to consider all your choices so you can buy the *right* car. What make, model, color, seating capacity, and accessories do you want?

In today's market, you have just as many choices shopping for a mortgage as you do picking out a car. Finding the one that best fits your needs depends on the amount of research you're willing to do. Just as you researched various cars before visiting a dealership, do the same with mortgage products. And pay special attention to the psychology of getting a loan.

First, realize that your loan officer, counselor, or broker (whatever name he or she uses) is a *salesperson* who sets out to earn the biggest commission possible. That's why it's critical to know your options. By presenting yourself as an educated consumer, you lessen your chances of being ripped off. Indeed, the more you know and the smarter you appear, the less likely you'll be taken for a ride.

Next, few people set out to "buy a mortgage." Instead, their mindset is to "get a loan" or "get financed." But if you have the passive mindset of someone *giving* you a loan, you put yourself at a disadvantage. Check that mindset at the door. You don't need to view this transaction as a big favor. The truth is this: The loan officer needs your business as much as you need the loan. So adopt a consumer mindset as the savvy buyer, the ultimate decision maker.

Shopping for Good Rates

Mortgage rates are determined through in-depth formulas based on numbers that consumers really don't need to understand. Bottom line, you just want to know what's the best rate available *for you* in your current situation, since the details vary a lot.

Mortgage rates are quoted in 0.125 increments or an eighth of a percentage point (e.g., 6.00, 6.125, 6.25, and 6.375 or 6, 6⅛, 6¼, and 6⅜). As you shop around, you check the rates on one particular day and find that various mortgage companies have different rates for the same type of loan. Why is this? Well, if you view buying mortgages like buying cars, how much you pay depends on where dealers purchase a particular car (e.g., from the manufacturer, used car auctions, wholesale, etc.). Dealers price their products according to the discounts received when they purchase the cars. This variation allows them to charge more or less money as their competitors do for the exact same vehicle.

The same is true for mortgages. Certain mortgage companies do a higher volume of sales in one product, allowing their lender (supplier) to sell it at a discount rate. That discount makes it easier for the mortgage company to sell that product to consumers for less. Your goal is to find the mortgage company that sells, in volume, the product you want to purchase—just like buying a car.

But I caution you, the interest rate is *not* the only thing to consider when purchasing a loan. Take into account rates, products, *and* fees, just as you'd consider different makes, models, and accessory packages for a car. Is there anything standard about fees? No, absolutely not. Although some fees are fixed—such as doc stamps on a deed, taxes, and title insurance—others are not. These include loan origination fees, discount fees, appraisals, credit reports, underwriting fees, processing fees, wire fees, and so on. These fees vary from lender to lender.

Along with shopping for a good source for your mortgage, also evaluate the total costs of the loan, including the interest rate, broker fees, points (each point is 1 percent of the amount you borrow), prepayment penalties, term of the loan, application fees, credit report fee, appraisal costs, and a host of other items. Just as the car salesman can rip you off by selling a worthless warranty, so can loan officers and mortgage brokers rip you off by charging junk fees at the closing table.

To protect yourself, there's one antidote: *Do your homework.* Conduct a thorough check of prospective mortgage brokers. Call their references. Only work with a good, honest, upright broker who has a proven track record. And only deal with a company that's been in business for at least three years.

When you're in the market for the best mortgage *for you,* the time you spend doing a thorough search will pay off in the long run.

EVALUATING LOAN PROGRAMS

You won't find a simple answer to the question "Which loan program should I use?" Answers vary tremendously. The right type of mortgage depends on these factors:

- Your current financial picture
- How you expect your finances to change
- How long you intend to keep your house
- How much you intend to rent your property for
- Your comfort level with your mortgage payment and the possibility of it changing
- Your intention to "rent by owner" or hire a management company (which means paying commissions)
- Your intention to pay the property off by paying down the principal or, alternatively, to rely on the property's appreciation to make you money

As you set out on this journey, remember this rule of thumb: The more risky it is for the bank or mortgage company to lend you money, the more you'll have to pay in interest rates and closing costs.

Length of the Loan

The term or length of the loan you buy can affect your bottom line in many ways. For example, buying a 22-year fixed-rate mortgage compared with a 30-year loan can save you thousands of dollars in interest payments over the life of your loan. However, with a shorter loan, your monthly payments are higher, making it more difficult to break even with your rental income. Also, paying out a higher dollar amount every month ties up more cash, thus making it more difficult to leverage your money. Getting an adjustable-rate mortgage might get you started with a lower monthly payment than a fixed-rate mortgage, thus making it easier for your property to pay for itself through rental income. But with this kind of loan, your payments will likely increase when interest rates go up.

When you're calculating mortgage products, I suggest getting comfortable using mortgage calculators. (Go to http://www.How ToRentByOwner.com for information.) Also know your goals and restrictions right from the day you purchase the loan. Set the term of your loan accordingly.

Qualification Guidelines

I suggest you consider these two separate qualification guidelines when purchasing each particular product: conforming and nonconforming loans. Although the products are basically the same, your qualification factors are different. For example, a conforming mortgage refers to the usual way to purchase a loan governed by rules set by industry standards (although program guidelines might still vary from lender to lender). Conforming loans generally require that your financial situation fit into government standards known as Fannie Mae and Freddie Mac guidelines. (For information on conforming loans figures and facts, go to http://www.HowToRentByOwner.com.) Beware. These guidelines may or may not include maximum loan amounts, certain debt-to-income ratios, and minimum credit scores.

Nonconforming mortgages apply when your situation or your property doesn't fit into a perfect box defined by conforming loan guidelines. If you need a huge loan, if your credit score is low, if your debt-to-income ratio is high, or if you're self-employed, you might be required to purchase through nonconforming guidelines. Generally speaking, you pay more because there is more risk for the lending institution that lends money to this group of people.

When determining how much you need to borrow, be sure to add in costs for furnishings and renovations. Plan ahead and don't get caught short when you can fold in a few more thousand into the loan to cover these expenses.

Down Payments and PMI

Most homebuyers face the challenge of coming up with a down payment. If everybody had socked away 20 percent of the purchase price in cash to put down on a vacation home, life would be simple. But today, you can overcome most obstacles to acquiring down payment funds through creative financing. There are even loans available for 100 percent financing, which means no down payment at all (see "Portfolio Financing" later in this chapter). Remember the days when lending companies probed into the source of your down payment and it was considered taboo to borrow it? Well, that's no longer true. Loan products specifically set up for that purpose are readily available.

Understand that many lenders require private mortgage insurance, or PMI, for loans exceeding the 80 percent loan-to-value range. Not only is PMI expensive, but also it can be deducted only for income tax purposes under certain investment property guidelines. (Be sure to check with your accountant or CPA before purchasing the loan to see if he or she thinks PMI costs are tax-deductible for you.) If you can't deduct PMI costs, then you're required to have the 20 percent down payment to avoid paying PMI, right? No! You can borrow those funds, too.

Mortgage brokers have yet another product called piggyback loans or 80/10/10 or 80/15/5 loans. Let's look at the 80/15/5 loan first. With this loan, you acquire a first mortgage for 80 percent loan-to-value and a simultaneous second mortgage for 15 percent. This kind of loan requires you to have a 5 percent down payment. The same applies for the 80/10/10 in which your first mortgage is 80 percent and you get a second mortgage of 10 percent, plus you must come up with the 10 percent down payment. While the second mortgage comes with a higher interest rate than your first mortgage, the elimination of the PMI insurance generally covers that difference.

> For a down payment, Caroline cashed in some stocks in her investment portfolio. Her reasoning? She expects her money to earn more in real estate than in the stock market. Then she purchased a 30-year fixed, second-home loan and opted to pay 1⅛ points higher in interest as a way to forgo paying PMI. Her calculations showed it was less expensive to take the higher interest rate than to pay PMI. Even though PMI would be a deductible business expense in her situation, the determining factor came down to cash flow; not paying PMI reduced her loan payment by $60 a month.

Creative Ways to Get Your Down Payment

You don't have to have huge amounts of money in the bank to get started as a vacation home owner. Mostly, you need to think creatively. For example, you can borrow against the equity in your primary home to get funds to start. I often suggest taking money you've accumulated in your property as equity and using it to purchase a vacation property. You could borrow it in the form of a second mortgage, a home equity line, a cash-out refinance, or even a reverse mortgage. (These are explained later in this chapter.)

Suppose you bought your house 15 years ago for $150,000. Today, it's worth $250,000 and your mortgage has been paid down to $100,000. That translates into $150,000 worth of equity in your home. You could use a portion of that to put a down payment on a vacation property. If, for example, you want to buy a cabin that costs $200,000, you'd need $20,000 to put 10 percent down or $40,000 to put 20 percent down. (You may or may not want to avoid paying PMI. Depending on how you set up your vacation rental, you could benefit from having a tax deduction against your vacation rental business. Check with your tax advisor to see what's appropriate in your situation.)

Another way to acquire a down payment is—how obvious—to save it. If that's difficult for you, follow the guidance of well-known financial gurus like Suze Orman and Clark Howard and learn ways of budgeting so you can save for that first down payment.

When I was in my 20s, I had a good-paying job and, although I wasn't wealthy, I was comfortable. About the same time, my cousin emigrated from a former Soviet republic. She and her husband came to the United States with nothing—no money or possessions at all. My father allowed them to live in one of his houses rent-free, and they both got minimum-wage jobs. By the end of five years of working hard, working two jobs each and lots of overtime, they had saved $30,000 to use as a down payment on their first home! In that same time frame, what did I have? Fun—in the form of a flashy car, nice clothes, and elaborate vacations. How did they save that much money (when I didn't)? They lived on a minimum budget and only spent what they had to. As I got older and wiser, I realized that some of the things I thought were important—the flashy car, fancy dinners and restaurants, and so on—were just not that meaningful to me. What really mattered was building a sound financial future.

Prequalifying and Preapproving

Fast-forward to the point when you're ready to buy a property and need a lender's agreement to approve a loan. What is the best way to approach the seller of the property you want to buy? You can get *prequalified* for a loan, but it's even better to come to the negotiating table armed with a *preapproval* letter. Let me explain the difference between the two.

Prequalification. In this case, you go to the loan officer and tell him or her your income and expenses. The officer punches a few numbers into the computer, probably runs a quick credit report, and then tells you how much you can afford to borrow. This verbal approximation comes with no guarantees that you will qualify for the loan.

Preapproved pending property. While prequalification can help you learn approximately how much you can afford, it doesn't offer the same advantages as actually being preapproved. In this situation, you've met with the loan officer for prequalification, and your files have been sent to processing and underwriting so you can become totally approved for a specific loan amount. With this approval in place, the lender waits for you to bring the sales contract on a property and then fills in the blank lines on the closing documents.

Why do this? Preapproval pending property is like having a blank check in your pocket waiting to be filled out! It gives you leverage as a buyer, whether your properties are in a seller's market or a buyer's market.

Because Cape Cod has been developed for nearly 300 years, there's no more available land to be purchased. Consequently, each time a property goes up for sale, ten or more buyers compete to purchase it. If you were the seller, would you sell to someone who doesn't have an approved loan in hand? Would you risk accepting an offer from a buyer who may not qualify for a loan? Or would you sell to the buyer who has already gone through the mortgage process and has full loan approval? Of course you would pick the sure deal.

If you're a buyer in a buyer's market, you can choose from dozens, maybe even hundreds, of properties for sale. During a buyer's market, homes have likely been on the market for long periods of time. With your preapproval in your pocket, you can go to the seller of the property you want and offer considerably less than the asking price. Use it as a negotiation factor that gives you a better chance of the seller accepting your offer.

I followed this advice when I purchased my first property in Destin, Florida, in 1997. First, I got preapproved for a loan, and then I looked at numerous properties priced within my preapproval dollar amount. I narrowed my choices to ten properties. My plan was to offer a low-ball price and keep going down the line until I found a seller who would take my offer. I put an offer on the first property and told the sellers that I could close in two weeks! (Back then, mortgages took four to six weeks to process—so two weeks was an astonishing amount of time.) I learned that the sellers didn't feel offended about the low-ball offer since the property had been on the market for more than six months, and two contracts had fallen through due to buyers not qualifying for the loan. The sellers made a counteroffer and I agreed to split the difference. I called the appraiser and inspector, asked if they could have the property ready to close in a week. The sellers, of course, went along with it. In the end, I purchased the property at 86 percent of the market value and closed in one week. This allowed me to start off with 14 percent equity in the property from day one. You might think that result is tough to beat—but I encourage you to try!

Think Like a Consumer

Think back to the last time you bought a car from a dealership. Did you pay the full asking price or consider buying only one car? No. You shopped around before signing on the dotted line. Because it's a much bigger purchase than an automobile, a mortgage has much more at stake, so don't be afraid to ask questions. Kick the tires, check with customers, and do comparison shopping. Chances are you'll find an excellent mortgage product that addresses your situation and your needs. But the best one won't leap into your arms; it's up to you to find it. Be a conscientious shopper.

FINANCING OPTIONS

How will you use your vacation home—as a second home or as an investment property? Determining your intention makes a difference in the kind of mortgage you should get. It also has significant income tax implications, which is an issue to discuss with your tax advisor.

As a rule, the Internal Revenue Service (IRS) expects that most vacation home owners will rent their property at least casually; the degree to which it's rented determines if it's a second home or investment property. (For a brochure on this subject, go to http://www.irs.gov/pub/irs-pdf/p527.pdf.)

To determine the answer, add the number of days you and your renters use the property. If it's fewer than 14 days a year or less than 10 percent of the days it's rented to outsiders each year (whichever is greater), then it's an investment property. If you use it 15 days or more, than it's considered to be a second home. That means if you declare it as a second home and collect 14 days of rental income, you don't pay taxes on it. But if it's an investment, you'd declare the income to deduct for business expenses on the home. The days you spend improving and maintaining the property do not count as part of the 14-day/10 percent test.

I suggest keeping track of these days with a guest book placed in the rental for visitors to sign. In the same book, log the dates and activities of your personal and work visits. This provides a record at tax time or if the IRS does an audit. (Go to http://www

.HowToRentByOwner.com to purchase a guest book that serves this purpose and many more.)

Second-Home Loans

When purchasing you'll find that interest rates for second-home loans are approximately the same as for a primary property mortgage, with a minimal down payment. Getting a second mortgage on a primary residence is my favorite way to purchase a vacation home because you won't incur "up charges" or higher rates.

This type of loan works exactly the same way as the loan on your primary residence works. Basically, if you made it through the loan process on your primary residence, then you can get through the process of a second-home mortgage. And for income tax purposes, you can convert your property from a second home to an investment property *after* you purchase the loan to help maximize your income tax deductions.

Be sure to read the fine print in your loan documents. Today, some mortgages come with clauses that state you have to occupy the premises for a certain amount of time for it to qualify as a second-home loan (as opposed to an investor loan). The only caveat is you must be able to qualify under the second-home's terms, which means you have to be able to show you can afford it just as you would your first home.

Please note that under the terms of this loan there is *no consideration for potential rental income.* That means if your primary residence mortgage is $250,000 and your second-home mortgage is $200,000, then you must to be able to qualify for $450,000 worth of debt. Therefore, if you've maxed out your debt on your primary residence, this isn't the loan option for you. But have no fear; there's a loan out there that will suit your needs.

When Caroline and Ken shopped for a loan, they found that because their debt-to-income ratio was low and they had a high credit score (800), they were able to qualify for a second-home loan. They had to pay close attention to all the stipulations within this loan to be sure they could rent out the home (which they could).

Investment Property Loans

With an investment property loan, everyone concerned knows you're buying the property strictly as an investment, so certain factors come into play. First, the lender wants to know the rental history of the property. Understand that because lenders consider investment loans to be higher risk than mortgages for your primary home, that risk translates into higher interest rates and higher fees. I suggest making your financial decisions based on your break-even formula calculation.

Years ago, my husband and I bought a condo for $34,000. As odd as it may seem, mortgaging a small amount of money is actually difficult to do, especially for a condo. At the time, the average interest rates for mortgages were 7 percent, and we had to pay 11 percent for this property. But right from the beginning, this rental property had positive cash flow, even considering we had to pay a high interest rate. We sold the condo two years later for $69,000, which was a $35,000 gain. If I had let a high interest rate dictate my decision to purchase, I would have missed out on earning $35,000. Thankfully, the up charges on interest for investment properties aren't as high today as they used to be.

ADDITIONAL FINANCING OPTIONS

Going back to an elementary level of financing, the most common options are fixed-rate and adjustable loans. These products have been available since the beginning of the time when mortgages became popular. I would venture to guess you've used these products yourself and are familiar with them. Most of us tend to stay in our comfort zones and make decisions based on what we already know.

But in today's market with money being so inexpensive to borrow, you can benefit from venturing outside your comfort zone. Consider other products available, such as interest-only loans, portfolio financing, and self-directed IRAs. These products allow you minimum cash out of your pocket on a month-to-month basis, thus letting you continue to use your cash flow to diversify your investments. Let me summarize all these options.

Fixed-Rate, Fixed-Term Mortgage

With this kind of mortgage, your interest rate and monthly payments don't change over the length of the loan. Property taxes and homeowners fees may increase, but otherwise your monthly payments remain stable.

You'll find that fixed-rate, fixed-term mortgages are available for 30 years, 20 years, 15 years, and even 10 years. Under a fixed-rate fully amortizing loan, a large percentage of the monthly payment goes to pay the interest during the early amortization period. As the loan is paid down, more of the monthly payment gets applied to principal. For example, a typical 30-year fixed-rate mortgage takes 22.5 years of level payments to pay off half of the original loan amount.

However, most investment advisors suggest buying a loan for an investment property for the longest term available because you're leveraging someone else's money instead of yours. Therefore, you can use your own money for other diversified investments.

Only go with this type of loan if it makes the most sense in your situation. I encourage you to take a look at the following options, too.

Portfolio Financing

Did you know that you could use your current stock portfolio to finance a property? Companies like Merrill Lynch, PaineWebber, and Morgan Stanley now make these products available to property investors. How? By using a portion of your portfolio as collateral.

This availability tells me that stock brokerage firms now realize that real estate is a viable investment means. Say you have $200,000 worth of stocks, bonds, annuities, and so on, in your investment portfolio. These companies will lend two to three times the amount of your portfolio to purchase real estate. That means having a $200,000 portfolio would allow you to purchase $400,000 to $600,000 worth of property. You can even purchase at 100 percent financing, no down payment required, and no cashing in your stocks.

You also can buy, sell, and defer capital gains on liquidated securities and still use pledged securities. Of course, you could run into a trading restriction on the collateralized stocks. Just remember that your mortgage interest may not be deductible if you're using tax-deferred stocks. In some cases, you can pay back the principal according to your own income schedule. Talk with your portfolio advisor about details that affect you.

Self-Directed IRAs

Are all of your stocks tied up in individual retirement accounts (IRAs)? Did you know that you could buy real estate, including vacation properties, with your IRA funds? Jeffrey Desich, a vice president with Equity Trust Company and registered principal with Mid Ohio Securities, is involved in both real estate and the financial services industry. This expert on real estate investing with self-directed retirement accounts says, "With a self-directed IRA, you have the ability to take control of your retirement savings. A self-directed IRA is an individual retirement account in which you call the shots and choose your own investments. By investing your IRA in real estate, you have the ability to shelter your profits from taxes. Both rental income and appreciation of the property grow either tax-deferred or tax-free!"

With these self-directed accounts, you have the ability to invest in stocks, bonds, mutual funds, and special assets like vacation properties. However, you must select a custodian for your self-directed IRA if you choose to use your IRA to purchase your property. When qualifying that person or company, make sure you ask these questions:

- Does this custodian offer one low flat fee with no hidden costs?
- Will he or she allow me to invest in nontraditional assets like vacation properties?
- Does he or she have experience and knowledge in real estate?
- Is the firm federally regulated?
- Will I have access to knowledgeable individuals and not an automated service?

Once your IRA owns the property, all expenses related to this investment will be paid from the funds in your self-directed IRA according to the directions you set up. In addition, all income made from the investment will be sent into your IRA, where it grows tax-deferred or tax-free depending on the account type.

Note: This program has strict guidelines. Be sure to consult with your financial advisor or tax attorney.

Jilean found an investment property she liked and decided to use her $150,000 self-directed IRA funds to finance it. Given that limit, she knew she couldn't exceed her budget, so she bought a home that was priced at $120,000. It was about $20,000 under comparable market value because of its outdated decor and shabby appearance. Funds from her self-directed IRA completely covered the purchase price plus renovations that cost $12,000. In her first year as a landlord, Jilean brought in $30,000 in rental revenue, which translates into a 20 percent gain on her initial investment of $150,000. Add to that a conservative appreciation of 10 percent and she realized a 30 percent gain on her IRA-funded investment in one year.

Reverse Mortgages

You could also set up a reverse mortgage, defined as a home loan that gives cash advances to a homeowner, requires no repayment until a future time, and is capped by the value of the home when the loan is repaid. (Go to http://www.aarp.org/revmort for more details.)

Rich and Julie have a combined family income of $70,000. Because of their good credit and ability to leverage money from their existing home, they were able to purchase a vacation home that cost $140,000. They put down 10 percent ($14,000) from funds that came from setting up a reverse mortgage and did a 30-year fixed mortgage for the remaining 90 percent ($126,000). From the get-go, they banked on this property paying for itself using a rent-by-owner formula. They're confident their plan will be a moneymaker over time.

Adjustable-Rate Mortgages

Adjustable-rate mortgages (ARMs) generally start with an interest rate that's 2 to 3 percent below a comparable fixed-rate mortgage and could therefore allow you to buy a more expensive home than a fixed-rate mortgage. However, the interest rate changes at specified intervals—every year, every three years, etc.—depending on changing market conditions. Understand that if interest rates go up, your monthly mortgage payment will go up, too, at some point. Conversely, if rates go down, your mortgage payment also will drop.

Some mortgages combine the characteristics of both fixed-rate and adjustable-rate mortgages starting at a low fixed rate for, say, seven to ten years, then adjusting the rate to changing market conditions.

Interest-Only Loans (Fixed and LIBOR)

Specific loans are tied to certain indexes. For example, LIBOR (London Interbank Offered Rate) is used as a base index for setting rates of some adjustable-rate financial instruments, including ARMs. Specifically in this case, the borrower gets a low interest rate like 3.25 percent. If you use this type of loan, you only pay the monthly interest payment amount; there is no principal payment. Consequently, you build no equity from your payments unless you make additional principal payments. This is a great loan for a property that will almost certainly appreciate in value over a short period of time.

With this loan, you're operating on a floating interest level, which is tied to fluctuating markets. It allows you to purchase the most expensive property that you might otherwise have never been able to afford.

Take, for instance, a loan amount of $750,000. With an interest-only LIBOR loan, the interest rate could be as low as 2.5 percent, making the payment only $1,562 a month. Compare that with a 30-year mortgage with a fixed rate at 5.5 percent, which would be $4,258 a month.

See the difference in how much more you could afford with this type of loan? This is a great product for people who intend on owning for short periods of time and "flipping" their properties. Mostly, the owners are straight investors who are banking on the property appreciating hugely. Of course, this more volatile loan is not for the weak of heart. And buyer beware, because it allows you to afford much more than you could under conventional mortgages. You don't want to get into debt way over your head.

Here are examples of how payments can differ depending on the product you choose. Given a mortgage amount of $150,000 and a conforming loan with no points or origination fees:

Product	Rate	Payment
30-year fixed	5.625%	$ 863
15-year fixed	5.00%	$1,186
1-year ARM	3.25%	$ 653
3/1 ARM	4.00%	$ 716
5/1 ARM	4.875%	$ 794
1-year LIBOR	2.25%	$ 281

Remember, don't think just because you want the "ultimate" in vacation properties, you can't start with one in a lower price range than the dream home you'll eventually have. It's just like buying the Honda you can afford now and the Lamborghini you *really* want later on.

"GOING IN" WITH FRIENDS AND FAMILY

To finance your vacation home, perhaps you want to go in on an investment property with friends or family members. This concept could work or it could backfire with disastrous results, so think carefully before forming an investment partnership. I know of several family members who don't speak to each other today because they unsuccessfully mixed "business" with "family." Having relationships you value with fellow investors can make life complicated when it comes to sorting out property issues. Lots of successful investors make joint ownership work well. Again, let me say that if you go in with others, please take all the necessary legal and personal issues into consideration. Hire an attorney to draw up legal documents that will cover your interests. Keep reading and see how following good management and investment ideas can help you plan for and deal with any sticky problems.

Seek Like-Minded Investors

Often you can buy properties jointly with other investors. These might be people you don't know yet or only know through business associations. Get in touch with Real Estate Investor (REI) groups in your community as a starting point and learn as much as you can through their experiences and advice. How do you find them? Probably the fastest way is by doing a search on the Internet.

Sandy, Thomas, and two other couples recently took the initiative to buy a vacation town house in a newly developed complex near a skiers' paradise in Colorado. Because they're all getting their feet wet in the vacation rental business at the same time, they're pooling their resources and learning how to manage the town house themselves. They're full of optimism about their partnership but also have legally formalized all their agreements to cover everyone's interests in this venture.

Again, don't shortchange yourself on getting legal advice. If you're going in with four other people, remember your legal expenses are only one-fifth of the entire amount, which is a benefit. All in all, joint venturing makes it more affordable and less risky.

Personal Stays and Joint Ownership

Be sure to consider all aspects of property ownership beyond financing before you leap ahead. That includes managing, furnishing, decorating, upkeep, and so on. Specifically, determine how you'd arrange personal stays equitably. What if you go in with your friend who wants to use the property four weeks a year, but you can only use it for one week? You need the rental revenue to pay your portion of the bills and she does not.

How can you handle scheduling problems? I suggest doing a drawing or lottery. Write down all dates of the peak weeks on pieces of paper, put them into a hat, and each of you draws the weeks you'll take responsibility for—and trading is allowed! Think of this in the same way you might share season tickets to Yankees games.

Gabe and Mike have joint ownership in a condo in Park City, Utah, where the peak season runs from November to March. Both of them wanted to use the condo at Thanksgiving and Christmas, so they put papers labeled with those two holidays in a hat and did a drawing. Gabe drew Thanksgiving and Mike drew Christmas. Then they put papers representing the rest of the peak weeks in a hat and each of them drew a certain number of weeks. For the weeks Gabe pulled out of the hat, he receives the revenue generated for those weeks. The same applies to Mike for his weeks.

Keep in mind that, with joint ownership, you can make up any rules you want—as long as you both agree.

Exit Strategy

How do you take into account everyone's interests when the joint ownership arrangement no longer works? It's best to *predetermine* an exit strategy that you all agree to. What happens if one party wants to get out and take the accrued appreciation, but the other can't afford to buy the original owner out? What dilemmas can arise?

I suggest answering these questions before moving forward:

- Can your legal partnership be sold?
- Can it be willed to a beneficiary?
- Can it be put in a trust?
- What happens if one of the partners dies? Will your property be held in probate?
- What happens if one of the partners gets divorced? Does the property become a factor in the divorce battle?

For some people, joint ownership is a great way to afford a place and minimize your risks. Still, the old adage, "Don't mix business with pleasure," needs to be seriously considered.

Two sisters, Judy and Helen, buy a place together. Each has four kids. Helen passes away and wills her ownership in the property to her four kids. All of a sudden, Judy now has to deal with four decision makers and their diverse opinions. In retrospect, they could have drawn up an agreement specifically defining what happens when either of the partners dies. That agreement would have curtailed this sticky situation from happening.

5

NEGOTIATING AN OFFER
AND CLOSING (FROM AFAR)

When making an offer on your vacation property, it's important for you and your real estate agent to be particularly savvy. After all, you assume you'll recognize the right property to buy in a heartbeat. It's easy to get caught up in a deal-making frenzy because, in most vacation destinations, prime properties get scooped up in a nanosecond—many of them even before a listing hits the Multiple Listing Service (MLS).

Experienced agents nurture customized lists of interested, viable clients and will contact them first when a desired property becomes available. A confident buyer knows each offer should be well thought out—price, location, amenities, and all that jazz—so he or she has some assurance that the buying decision made in a nanosecond is the right one!

What happens when the right property for you comes on the market? It's easy to get bamboozled by an agent pushing for a quick sale. And if you hesitate, you need to have a good, solid reason. Ask yourself, "What's the worst thing that can happen if I don't spring to action on this property?" Well, the second-worst thing is that someone else beats you to the contract-writing table. You lose the chance to buy the property. But even worse—the first-worst thing—is that you could end up owning a property that doesn't meet your criteria, one that doesn't fit your needs and could drain your finances, too.

Let's say you know exactly what you want, and like magic that property shows up. Yes, by all means, put a contract on it. But in your haste to return to your home city or placate your agent, don't get sloppy. Don't sign a blank contract as you rush away and trust your agent to complete it to your satisfaction. It's not wise to put that burden on your real estate agent. Do expect your agent to do research for you, but then confirm what you've been told as best you can. In particular, be sure to check community codes (either yourself or have your agent research them), then base your decision on up-to-date, correct information.

> Angela and Dick located a vacation property in a town where lots of people posted signs and rented their places by the week. When their agent called the local sales tax office to find out about their obligation to pay taxes, she also learned that the codes restricted short-term rentals. They required a minimum 30-day rental. When the couple heard that, it didn't matter that other vacation home owners did business on a week-by-week basis. They simply didn't want to go against the code. Even though they loved this property, they decided not to buy it.

THINK AHEAD NO MATTER WHAT

You're always challenged to find the balance between how quickly a property you like will sell and how close it comes to meeting your criteria for a vacation home. Think of this process as selecting classes at university: maybe you have to compromise in your choices. But you must make sure the overall selection of choices at the university suits your needs in the long run. Then, if you can't enroll in your first-choice classes, you can fall back on your second choices quite happily. The point is to leave open your future options. For example, if you set out to buy a second home for yourself, then circumstances change and you have to rent it out to cover expenses, make sure the place you buy covers both scenarios.

You can't be sure what the future will bring. Even though you may not purchase a vacation home to rent out today, it's a fallback strategy if you ever need additional income.

Sally and Bill never planned to rent out their vacation home when they bought and paid for it 30 years ago. However, when they retired, not only did their income decrease, but the New York State government significantly increased property taxes on both their primary and second homes. They now rent out their vacation home during the peak rental season to cover their tax bill; it was the only way they could afford to keep it.

Budget for Enhancements

Factor in extra money when you buy the property you've selected to make it aseptically pleasing and fresh looking for your rentals. Even though it's purchased as a turnkey rental, I always spend $1,000 to $2,000 to bring the furnishings up to a higher standard than I found them. In fact, I've planned that cost into my finances in the early stages of purchasing the property.

A cabin I purchased as a vacation rental accommodates six people, but the sellers had only a minimum number of utensils in the household: six knives, six spoons, six forks. There was no iron or ironing board; the beds were okay but uncomfortable. So adding to the cutlery and replacing the mattresses came out of the furnishing budget. Because I'd set aside funds for this purpose, I had no hesitation spending money to upgrade the furnishings and take care of extra details.

When a rental property changes hands, the bedding and towels usually don't come with it because they belong to the management company that takes care of the place. So I know that I will buy fresh sheets and towels out of the budget I set aside for furnishings.

> I *had to buy six sets of sheets for three beds in the new cabin because I knew I'd need enough for a quick turnaround. I bought 12 sets of towels, a broom, dustpan, mop, and cleaning solutions. Even though housecleaners have their own when they come in to clean, I never mind spending money on cleaning supplies. It makes it convenient for vacationers to keep up with spills, and I don't spend a moment worrying about them stealing the Windex. Convenience is critical!*

I also buy tools and supplies at the dollar store: hammer, nails, and electrical tape. And if the bed covers look old and dingy, it's easy to find new quilts and curtains at Wal-Mart or Target. Having old bedding not only looks tacky in the publicity photos you'll need for marketing, but it also could mean the difference between people renting or passing in favor of a place that looks prettier than yours.

I also make a point of giving the property a fresh coat of paint to add lots of curb appeal and recommend you do, too. Don't let a property's dingy look deter you; just be sure to budget for a cosmetic upgrade when you crunch the numbers.

NEGOTIATING THE DEAL

Have you noticed that, in our culture, at least *some* people tend to be uncomfortable with negotiating? My friends say, "Christine, you're the only person I know who stands in the pouring rain and dickers with the umbrella seller to get a cheaper price." My theory is always: It never hurts to ask. Many people simply won't ask for a better price.

Price Factor

At times, certain vacation properties are in such high demand that there's little room for negotiation. This is when your hard work in sourcing a good agent really makes a difference. Working with an agent who knows the territory well can be your ace. (Of course, it's important to remember that both agents—buyer's agent and seller's agent—are working on a commission based on the sales amount, so it's in their interest to get as much for the property as possible.)

One of my favorite negotiating tactics is this: I never disclose what I'm willing to pay for a property—even to my own agent. I want my agent to negotiate to the best of his or her ability for the lowest price. In their negotiations, some people would say, "If I can't get this property for $140,000, I won't buy it." But when I purchased my two cabins, I started offering $135,000 for each. My agent knew I'd go up to $140,000 each and thought that was my top-line number. But in my mind, I had decided I'd go as high as $150,000. I didn't tell him that, though, because I wanted him to negotiate for the amount that *he* believed was my absolute top offer.

Although price tends to be the number one negotiating factor, additional factors enter into the picture as this example showed. Certainly such factors as assessments, timing, furnishings, and trade-outs can influence a sale.

Assessment Factor

With vacation properties, you and your agent may run into special assessments that can be negotiated. For example, in Florida, many properties in condo complexes were damaged by the hurricanes of 2004. Under these circumstances, it would not be unusual for the association board of the complex to assess owners thousands of dollars to pay for repairs. Owners who simply could not afford to pay the assessment would have little choice but to sell their condos. Buyers interested in the condos would want to make a purchase with minimal cash outlay. Of course, they would expect to make a down payment and pay closing costs, but they would resist paying a special assessment. (Note: In some states, there may be laws stating it's the seller's responsibility to pay the special assessment before closing.)

Consequently, special assessments can become a point of negotiation in several ways, but here are three possible options:

1. The buyer could say to the seller, "I will buy your property *only* if you pay the special assessment."
2. The buyer could say to the seller, "I will buy your property if you agree to split the special assessment."
3. The buyer could say to the seller, "I will buy your property for $XX more than the asking price if you pay the special assessment." (By upping the sales price, the buyer funds the special assessment, provided the property will appraise for the additional amount.)

Timing Factor

Timing can be an important factor. For example, Caroline wanted to close the deal on her cabin during the high-rental season so she could get the lion's share of the rental revenue during that period. The original closing date was scheduled for October 30, but the seller agreed to close earlier if Caroline would honor the seller's first two weeks of bookings. That still left her with a two-week window in the month for finding her own renters. This proved to be a strong incentive for both the buyer and seller to finalize their deal.

The Matthews, an elderly couple who had lived as snowbirds in their second home for years, had just arranged to move into an assisted living center in their home state. A young couple, Larry and Linda, learned in early December that the Matthews's home would go on the market after Christmas. This happened to be a pretty tight market, with most homes selling for their exact asking price. They wanted to put in an offer but their agent said that the Matthews had set a firm price of $196,000, with no room for negotiation. In talking with the Matthews's agent, though, they found out that the sellers cared more about being able to stay in their home until the end of the winter season, as they usually did. By agreeing to a closing date of March 31 in their offer of $192,000, Linda and Larry knew they'd have a good chance to buy the home for less than the asking price. The compromise price of $193,500 made it a win-win situation.

Vacation Time Factor

Negotiations can take the form of rental time rather than money. Marian had a home she loved in a resort community, but when she got married, she moved into her new husband's home in a different community. When she sold her home, she negotiated with the buyers to spend a week rent-free every year for the following five years as a condition of the sale. What a difference that made to her in feeling good about the transaction.

Furniture Factor

Even if the home is listed as "unfurnished," do some detective work to find out what the sellers plan to do with the furnishings. Will they be having an estate sale to move items they don't want? Be sure to ask. Try to factor in any furniture you want with other negotiation points, such as price, timing of the close, or other trade-offs. If you don't ask for what you want, you'll never get it! With creative thinking, you can help turn a seller's desire to get rid of certain furnishings and supplies into a bonus for you.

I remember when our family moved from New York to Atlanta, we sold our home unfurnished. However, I had a lot of pieces I was willing to leave behind; I certainly didn't want to move them. In retrospect, I wish I had offered them for sale to the buyers.

DEALING WITH PAPERWORK FROM AFAR

When it comes to making offers on a second home, sending faxes back and forth makes it possible to finalize the details of the purchase long distance. However, when too many faxes with changes go back and forth, insist that the final negotiated offer be rewritten. If you don't, you're in danger of being asked to sign a totally illegible document that wouldn't stand up in a court in case of a dispute.

I suggest you ask for original documents to be signed by both buyer and seller within 48 hours of finalizing the details. In fact, demand that your offer be contingent on receiving original documents. I know of a situation in which the sellers backed out of a deal because things changed during the negotiation process. Because no one had a legible signed copy, the details of the agreement couldn't be deciphered.

A good real estate agent should willingly rewrite the contract so that both buyer and seller each hold one legible copy of the contract that has been signed by all appropriate parties.

Put Everything in Writing

If you find a vacation home on the resale market, most likely it will be sold fully furnished. Beware of the "illusions" you might have when you're drawn to buying a property that's furnished.

Often, during the walk-through of the property, you'll see beautiful furnishings. But what will you do if you find out after closing that the beautiful furnishings have been replaced with thrift-store finds, or the original artwork has been replaced with cheap prints? Though this doesn't happen often, you'll want to guard against that.

Real estate agent Shannyn Stevenson, in Destin, Florida, recommends taking photographs when you look at a property and keeping those photos handy as evidence in case there's a dispute. When you put in a contract, be sure to ask if all the furnishings are included and write the items into the contract.

In an MLS listing, you may see "fully furnished except for a few of the owner's personal belongings." But what does "few" really mean? Do "personal belongings" refer to the underwear in the drawer or the dining room table and the bedroom suite? In your contract, I suggest you request specifics about "owner's personal belongings." You can never be too detailed. Even if your agent looks at you cross-eyed, stand your ground and put everything in writing. When the seller signs the offer, make sure those blanks are filled in.

Once you decide you want to put an offer on a property, you or your real estate agent should take photos of every wall and show what's in every cupboard. It's not unusual to provide an inventory list. Some savvy buyers even take the inventory list to the next level of detail and include model numbers. The message is: Don't be trusting and naïve. This is a business deal, so put all the details in writing.

PREPARING FOR CLOSING AND THE CLOSING ITSELF

Assuming you've hired an expert to inspect your property (see Chapter 6) and you've been through the financing process, it's time for the final walk-through before sitting down at the closing table.

If it's at all feasible, I recommend that you do the walk-through yourself. You're the one signing on the bottom line; you're responsible for paying the mortgage. Although agents and inspectors can facilitate a lot of activity, you're the one ultimately responsible. So bite the expense bullet, make the trip, and be there for closing in person. It's much easier to negotiate *before* everyone has received their money than afterward.

When You Can't Be There

That said, if you simply can't be at the closing table, be sure to have a list of specific items you want your agent to verify. Keep in mind, the agent's idea of "fixed" might be different from your idea. And you're the one who has to live with the imperfections. Under these circumstances, have your agent call you from the property at the time of the final walk-through. You need copies of the contract, the inspection report, and photographs in hand. Have your agent check everything on your list of concerns in real time while on the phone with you.

When I arrived at my cabins in Gatlinburg just before the closing, I was dismayed to discover the deck railing, which was 45 feet off the *ground, hadn't been fixed to my satisfaction and was still unstable. This was something I had pointed out when I originally viewed the property. The sellers "fixed" the railing and both my agent and the seller's agent checked on the repairs for me. I was more than surprised to find out that their view of "fixed" completely differed from mine. Had I not taken the time to be present at the closing, I would have been left to pay for these repairs. We still went to the closing table, but we arranged to put funds in escrow to repair the railing correctly so the repair didn't hold up the closing for me or the seller. After the repairs were completed and inspected by both real estate agents and me, the money got dispersed to the contractor and the deal was completed. (Some repairs call for setting up a second home inspection. If you ask for major repairs to the furnace, roof, or anything structural that potentially costs a lot of money, it's worth the extra $200 to have the property inspected a second time. See Chapter 6.)*

I recommend doing your final walk-through within 72 hours of closing or, ideally, right before closing. That's when you look carefully at the requested repairs and furniture items, making sure they are "as advertised" with no substitutions. If you discover that something is not acceptable, you have the legal right to demand resolution before closing, or you can strike a compromise and use dollars to compensate for any changes in value.

Once you've completed your final walk-through and have your inspection report in hand, then the physical aspect of closing can be done by mail, by signing all documents in front of a notary. If your spouse is co-owner and can't be at the closing, it's possible to have an attorney write up a temporary "limited power of attorney," which authorizes you to sign papers on behalf of both of you.

When Renters Are on the Premises

If you're buying a property that's an established vacation rental property, you may have to deal with renters on the premises during many steps of the process—from the first look at the property to the inspection stage to the final walk-through. Do your best to respect the renters' privacy and rights to occupy that property, but remember, you're still responsible to make sure all repairs take place. If you cannot get into the property to do your final walk-through, I recommend putting funds in escrow (to cover any items that were agreed to be repaired) until you or your representative (your agent or inspector) signs off on the requested repairs. If the seller won't agree to this procedure, you might consider walking away. Remember, if you sign the closing document and repairs are outstanding, you're taking on the responsibility for these repairs yourself.

For the most part, it should be easy to have access to the property, even when renters live there. If they object, there are always some sugar-and-spice ways to entice them. The agents, or you, can treat them to dinner out so you can complete a walk-through to your satisfaction.

6

HOME INSPECTIONS AND INSURANCE

If home ownership is rightly referred to as the American Dream, then owning a vacation home must be heaven. And if the majority of expenses are paid by others when you're not using the home, that's close to divine. But should unknown, undiscovered, or undisclosed defects exist, your perfect dream may rapidly become a nightmare.

How do you minimize the risk of the unknown? By inspecting the home before you buy it and insuring it afterward, you guard against loss from future problems. Also use title insurance to make sure the title to the property you want to buy is "free and clear" of any ownership questions.

WHAT IS A HOME INSPECTION?

(This section on home inspections was written by Wallace J. Conway, author of Secrets of the Happy Home Inspector: Your Guide

to a Comfortable and Confident Inspection Experience *and is used with permission here.*)

A home inspection is like a physical exam for your home. The mind-set of your home inspector is similar to that of your family doctor. The inspector, much like your doctor, looks for symptoms that would indicate problems. When a symptom is seen, the challenge is to determine its cause and prescribe a remedy.

Commonly, your choice in buying resort property is unlike buying your primary residence. For that reason, it's critical that your home inspector has extensive and specific knowledge of the factors influencing your new home's construction and care. It is likewise critical that your inspector has substantial experience inspecting homes that are similar in age and style to the one you want to purchase.

Take climate issues, for example. They affect homes in Vail differently from those in Palm Beach. People in Palm Beach don't care about ice damming unless it clogs their daiquiri machines! Likewise, visitors to Vail seldom worry about hurricane tie-down requirements. Your inspector's first job is to know what climate issues in your area affect the home you've selected.

Certainly, the years spent inspecting thousands of beachfront condominiums have little application to mountaintop cabins. In these two examples, every system is different. The roof on the cabin may be constructed of wood shakes, while the roof of the condo is most likely flat and made of rubber. The cabin is likely heated with a wood stove, while the condo is heated by a commercial-grade steam system. In many cases, the only common element is the microwave oven! Be sure to ask for specific experience when choosing your inspector.

Choose Your Inspector Now!

Consider the merits of selecting your home inspector even before you select a vacation home to buy. It's similar to lining up your financing in advance. When you know who to hire and trust that person is experienced and available, things will go more pleasantly. "Pleasant" is always good in a real estate transaction, but it's especially important when the primary purpose of the property is your rest and relaxation.

By identifying the inspector you want to work with, that person becomes a great education resource during the selection process. You'll have questions regarding different issues on competing properties; why not have an expert on call to educate you to your best decision? It will certainly boost your confidence in the buying process.

Both before and during the inspection, it's not about what details the inspector *learns* about a home, but rather what information he or she can *give you* about it. That information helps you both in the purchase decision and in the home's long-term care.

Ask lots of questions. Your inspector can provide answers in the context of your home, its location, and your own home experiences as a frame of reference. It's simpler and more comfortable to make buying decisions when you feel properly informed.

My Agent's Desires

Often the question is asked, "Should I accept the inspector recommended by my real estate agent?" The simple answer is yes, no, and maybe. Yes—if you choose an agent who has experience with dozens of homes similar to your choice, there is no conflict of interest between agent and inspector, and you trust your agent implicitly, then consider the recommendation. No—if your agent is new to the business, unfamiliar with similar properties, or you do not feel implicit trust. Maybe—for you can seek recommenda-tions from your agent as a starting point. Ask your agent these questions about the inspector or inspectors recommended:

- Do you have any business or personal relationships with this inspector?
- How many similar transactions have you been in with this inspector?
- Have you used this inspector on any of your personal real estate purchases?

With this information, visit the inspector's Web site, call with questions, and verify credentials. At this point, you can make a comfortable selection.

Is it always necessary to go to this level of detail? In truth, no! In fact, it's seldom necessary. But you won't know if you should have been this diligent until it is too late. So do the work now, then rest at your new resort home when it's done!

Finding a Credible Inspector

What credentials should your inspector have to ensure the highest probability of a happy home inspection experience? The number one credential is the inspector's membership in the Amer-ican Society of Home Inspectors (ASHI). Founded in 1976, this or-ganization is the oldest, largest, and most respected professional organization for the education and certification of home inspec-tors. It represents more than 6,000 home inspectors spread across the country in 80+ chapters.

ASHI has defined a strict Code of Ethics, a well-defined Stan-dards of Practice, and the most demanding membership certifi-cation requirements in the country. In those states that regulate home inspectors, the specific rules established by the state must be respected. Additional education requirements of independent professional organizations can only serve to improve the inspector's ability to serve the public. The majority of regulated states developed their regulations with strong input from ASHI. Many states folded under political pressure to establish state standards for testing and practical professional experience that were below the ASHI minimums. However, in other states, merely holding a license doesn't give consumers much assurance that the home inspector knows anything about inspecting homes. I suggest you study the license requirements for your state and certification requirements of professional organizations before making the choice to hire a home inspector. (A complete description of individual state licensing requirements is available online at http://www.ASHI.org.)

Other national associations also exist to serve inspectors. Some have high standards, and some low. Remember, credentials matter and so does experience. Inspectors simply stating they are "certified" or "licensed" means little. As a consumer, you must be informed to be protected.

Your Inspector Wants YOU!

More often than not, vacation homes are purchased a distance from your primary residence. This makes great sense. If you wanted to take a vacation in your hometown, you could just as easily stay home! But, this often complicates the inspection process.

It's always in your best interest to attend the home inspection yourself. Yes, you certainly receive a full written report, but nothing substitutes for being there. Those few hours together with your inspector can answer your questions, explain findings, and give a sense of comfort with your decisions that is near impossible to obtain from a distance. Having a home inspection without attending is like having your next physical exam via the telephone.

If you absolutely can't attend the inspection, insist on a call from your inspector while he or she is still at the house. That allows the inspector to snap an extra photo for clarity or check a last-minute item that may come to mind. This call will make the written inspection report simpler to understand when it arrives.

After you receive and review your report, be sure to follow up if you have even the slightest question in your mind about any of the report findings. More than one buyer has come away unhappy due to confusion, misunderstanding, or improper interpretation of an inspection report.

Don't worry about using the inspector's time or appearing unknowledgeable because of questions. Your inspector would prefer spending time discussing your concerns *before* you have a problem than afterward.

The Problem with Perfection

To be happy with a home, even a home with flaws, it's important to settle on reasonable expectations for inspecting the home. Determine by which standard it should be judged.

Of course, a common, though problematic, standard on which to form the basis of expectation is the standard of "perfection." It's easy to see how this thought gets into the minds of some home-buyers. Most people want to buy a particular home to get rid of some imperfection in their existing living quarters. It may be as simple as having outgrown the previous home or wanting to be closer to work. For the first-time buyer, it simply may be the idea of home ownership. But for a collection of reasons, buyers usually believe the physical condition of the home should be perfect.

But let's face it. There are *no* perfect houses! And if you attempted to build one that was perfect, no one would agree on what "perfect" really meant. And the cost would be exorbitant!

I have a saying, "Houses are like spouses. There are no perfect choices, but the consequence of a poor choice can be miserable." (Not to mention, expensive!) As you are recovering from that previous sentence, really think about it. This saying is the ultimate standard by which to judge houses!

"New" Be the Judge

Let's consider the idea of judging every home against a home built today. This seems like an ideal idea. When speaking to groups of both consumers and agents, I find that they initially agree this is a reasonable standard. But when it's considered against specific examples, the idea loses its luster.

Imagine a charming home built during the 1930s, perhaps a bungalow in the Arts and Crafts style. Among other fabulous details, it has glistening hardwood floors, detail moldings on every ceiling, and original brass fixtures lighting every room. To those who have an eye for such things, this home is gorgeous! But wait—what about those ungrounded electrical receptacles and asbestos shingles on the roof? Surely, those are a problem?

Yes, people want to know *if* they have problems! This is why they have regular physical exams and take their cars to the mechanic for inspections at prescribed mileages. People simply don't want to *have* problems. But, back to real estate, what is a problem?

Since the dawn of the real estate contract, lawyers and agents have sought to define problems in homes so they don't become obstacles to the contractual issues in closing the deal. Most efforts by lawyers and agents attempt to list (by including or excluding) those issues that most commonly disrupt deals in a specific locale.

But this approach to managing problems was developed to expedite the contract, not reflect the fears and needs of the parties involved. That is to say, if you're working with items that the contract says are "problems," it's unlikely both the buyer and the seller would judge the same list in a similar way.

Ask for What You Want

I'm always amazed at what you can get when you ask! While contracts and experience might indicate that a particular request has no chance of being granted, there's only one certainty—if you don't ask, you won't get anything.

I have known buyers to get everything from new carpet to tropical fish included in the deal, simply by asking. These requests have been most successful when they were part of the original offer. Sometimes, the request has resulted in a higher sales price, which never bothers the agents. And on other occasions, especially those requests dealing with personal property, that portion of the deal happened outside the bounds of the contract. Just be sure to include every desire in your original offer.

For example, many contracts have attempted to address the issue of "fogged windows." This "fogging" occurs when the seal is disrupted between the glass of double pane windows. Everyone agrees it's an unsightly discoloration, but few agree on if it's only a "cosmetic" condition. If deemed cosmetic, it's expected that the seller correct the problem. If deemed a more substantial issue, though, the buyer would be expected to find a remedy for solution within the repair or inspection section of the contract. It's best to address this situation in the original offer rather than waiting for the home inspection. It can become a tool for later negotiation.

During the negotiation process, there tends to be a desire to reduce the number of items repaired. If items identifiable by the homebuyer before the home inspection aren't included in the original offer, there may be no other opportunity to address those items. Always include in the original offer any known, disclosed, or observed items for repair. It makes the deal simpler. Always include the buyer's every desire in the original offer. You can't always get what you don't ask for, and sometimes you can't get what you don't ask for *early.*

(A note from Christine: Learn from my mistakes, even if your real estate agent doesn't agree, remember—it's *your* contract. Take Wally's advice here and insist!)

To Define and Prevent

Every list I have made attempting to completely address "problems" for correction by the seller has *failed.* By their nature, lists seek to include and exclude. They include for consideration only those items on the list, which, by default, excludes from consideration items not on the list. Lists, quite simply, always fail us! The answer lies in a simple and succinct definition of what a "problem" is!

Lawyers would say a problem is "something not functioning as intended." I love this definition. It is simple. It is succinct. And it works in every example or situation.

Let's revisit the issue of ungrounded electrical outlets—the ones with two holes for the plug prong instead of the prescribed three-hole outlets. Are they really a problem? Every time I ask this question, most people say "Yes." I can understand why someone would think that two-hole outlets are a problem, because these outlets lack a third hole for the ground wire of most modern appliances. This lack of grounding does increase the potential for both electrical shock and electrical damage to equipment. The two-hole ungrounded outlets do *not* meet present requirements of the National Electrical Code. Surely, so this is a problem.

Let's go back to our definition of a problem: "something not functioning as intended." If when the home was built, the electrical system was installed to meet the existing electrical code, and the system—in this case, the ungrounded electrical outlet—remains in its original configuration and is functioning as intended, is this by our definition a problem?

NO! If the outlet functions as intended, then it is not a problem. Should it be correctly disclosed, described, and documented as an ungrounded electrical outlet? Certainly, but to put it in simple terms, "If it ain't broke, don't fix it!"

THE NEED FOR INSURANCE COVERAGE

Don't overlook the importance of insurance and understanding why homeowners need to have it. If your vacation home or condo is part of an association, investigate to see if the association has a master insurance policy or a blanket policy that covers the common grounds and insures the exterior walls of the building (generally up to the drywall). If the building that houses your condo is covered by such a policy, you likely won't be required by your mortgage company to purchase separate insurance. Still, in my opinion, I think it's wise to consider buying added coverage. Blanket policies often do not provide coverage for everything *inside* your property (such as the cabinets, fixtures, and so on).

Also consider purchasing extra insurance if your property is located in an area that is at high risk for natural disasters such as hurricanes or floods. Proximity to the ocean or lakes can affect your risk. Yes, flood and hurricane insurance can get expensive, so research your options carefully.

When shopping for a new property, I considered buying a place that was right on the beach—until I found out that hurricane insurance for that home cost $3,600 a year. By contrast, insurance for a property right across the street from it cost only $600 a year. This proved to be a huge consideration when deciding to purchase this vacation home.

Personal Liability and Rental Insurance

In addition to homeowners or property insurance, consider purchasing personal liability insurance. Often, you can select this option as a rider policy on your current homeowners insurance as an extension of liability on your second home. This is important because, in today's overly litigious society, what happens if your renter falls in the shower and declares that his or her injuries were caused by some problem in the home? Then this could be viewed as your fault, and the issue could turn into an expensive legal battle. Insurance protects you from that.

Also, look into a specialized kind of policy known as rental insurance that covers your property in case you have a loss of rental income revenue due to events such as floods, fires, and so on. The cost for this kind of insurance is, in my opinion, too high to justify and I don't carry it on my properties. However, you might feel more secure purchasing insurance to cover a wide range of possibilities. Get educated right from the beginning and make good decisions for your circumstances.

DETERMINING THE RIGHT INSURANCE FOR YOUR VACATION HOME

Your primary residence is located in one area of the country and you're buying a second home in another area. What do you need to know about different insurance needs in different areas? What types of insurance are available?

Depending on where your vacation home is located, you should consider buying policies covering the following:

- Wind damage
- Flood damage
- Owner-occupied versus non-owner-occupied

It's difficult to find insurance specifically for vacation rental usage, though a few companies are now coming out with policies for this niche.

Remember, offering a home for short-term rental means you are in business—the business of providing an expensive asset to your customers. While your rentals may be booming, your rental income may be disproportionately low compared to the value of the real estate you allow guests to use. When you do your homework, you may be surprised to learn that everyday property and casualty insurance on your primary policy is not designed for rentals; therefore, it can be inadequate to protect your property. That means your current insurance carrier may disallow claims relating to incidents with renters. Indeed, the carrier may cancel your coverage with little warning if there is ever a claim, or it simply won't allow coverage of guests. This could leave you holding the bag for thousands of dollars.

Even if you think you're properly covered, you'd be wise to take a second look. Here's a general rule of thumb: Avoid taking risks that could cause you to lose your home or dramatically affect your finances.

ACQUIRING TITLE INSURANCE

No doubt you had to deal with title insurance experts when you bought your primary residence, but what does your dollar actually pay for when you purchase a title policy? You're really paying to eliminate the risk that the seller doesn't legally own the property and can't sell it to you.

The company title experts look at the chain of title of a home. They work backward, tracing every owner back to the point when the land was originally granted or sold from the local or federal government to the original owners. If a title has been recorded correctly, they can trace the lineage of a piece of land back to when that area was first settled.

People who work in title companies collect, store, maintain, and analyze official records of information that affects title to property. They're trained to identify the rights others may have in your property, such as recorded liens, legal actions, disputed interests, rights of way, or other encumbrances on your title. Before you can close on buying your property, you rely on the title company to "clear" any encumbrances you don't want to assume. In effect, they identify and eliminate potential risks or claims before they can happen.

Of course, you want clarity of the title for your own peace of mind, but your lender will certainly insist on having a title insurance policy in an amount that covers the loan. The lender also wants to know if there have been any liens (a claim made against a property by a person or tax assessor for the payment of a debt), or judgments (by a court of law), or easements (rights of others to use a portion of your land) filed against the property. Since the property itself serves as the lender's collateral against the loan, having a clear title to that property is essential.

Paying for Title Insurance

The rates you pay for this service vary from company to company. Behind the scenes, your policy premium pays for skilled personnel, data processing, title plant maintenance, research, evaluation, and legal interpretation.

Getting title insurance requires paying a one-time premium when you close the real estate transaction, compared with other kinds of insurance (e.g., health, homeowners, automobile, etc.) that require regular premium payments to keep the policy in force. Title companies also provide customer services to buyers, sellers, real estate developers, builders, mortgage lenders, and others who have an interest in real estate transfer.

People can take title insurance for granted, until the day they find out they really don't have it.

Shannon bought a condominium in Florida. On the MLS, it stated that the asking price included a designated covered parking space. Thankfully, when she signed the contract, she had a savvy agent who wrote the parking space into the contract. When she closed on the property, she purchased title insurance. But a vital loophole got overlooked (human error) when the attorneys filed the deed on the property. They forgot to include the title to the parking space in the deed!

A few months later, the previous owner sold the same parking space to another buyer, claiming that it was never part of Shannon's sale. She filed a claim on her title insurance policy and did win, but if she didn't have that title insurance, she would have lost her parking space.

People often don't realize that title insurance also protects the buyer from past liens on the property. In one situation, a housing development had a less-than-honest developer who built the homes but never paid the subcontractors. Consequently, the developer went bankrupt. The subcontractors' only recourse for compensation was to file liens against the properties that the developer owned. In the interim, the properties were sold to buyers. Because the closings and the liens happened almost simultaneously, the liens didn't show up in the title search of the properties. Bottom line—people who purchased title insurance were protected against the liens on their properties; those who did not were financially responsible for those liens.

I always recommend that you purchase title insurance!

DEEDED ACCESS

When purchasing property, people also can overlook the issue of deeded access. From the Web site http://www.Lectlaw

.com, the definition of deed is: "A written document for the transfer of land or other real property from one person to another." Therefore, in my interpretation, deeded access is a written and filed right to have access to a certain property. It gives you assurance that you have the right to use the land. Deeded accesses are especially important to vacation property owners.

For example, if you purchase a property that has beach rights, that means you have the right to get to the beach via that particular piece of land. But the "right," if not filed with the courts, can be discontinued by the grantor. Deeded beach access, however, means that you have legal rights to use that land forever.

The owners of a condominium complex along the beach in Destin, Florida, had acquired beach rights through another complex's land. One day, the complex managers decided they would no longer grant these beach rights. With no deeded beach access, the owners of the condominium lost a valuable asset–the right to use the beach. Now the owners and their guests have to drive to a public beach a couple miles away.

Here is an extreme case. Bob owned a property in Colorado. It was situated on five acres of land, but the land surrounding his property was owned by another landowner. The only way Bob could access his property was on a driveway through the other person's property. Even though this agreement had been made many years ago, they never got the access deeded "on the books." After that, the property surrounding Bob's was sold to another owner.

A year later, a forest fire burned down Bob's home. His insurance covered the loss, but during the process of pulling permits to rebuild his property, he learned that he needed to obtain right of access to his property from the new property owner. He came to find out the new owner would not allow access, leaving Bob with a worthless piece of property because he could only access it via helicopter.

PROFIT STRATEGIES

7

HOW TO RENT BY OWNER

Deciding whether it's wise to purchase a vacation home largely depends on the calculations you do to determine your break-even point—the point at which your income meets expenses. Calculating your break-even point helps you determine if you're likely to make a profit from owning a vacation property, coupled with the tax benefits that come with it.

One definition of your break-even point is having the property's income (rent) pay all the bills associated with the property. That means owning it shouldn't cost you anything out of your pocket after you make the initial down payment and furnish it for rentals.

Now, most financial analysts would say that breakeven is the point at which your income equals your initial investment and includes factors such as investments, depreciation, tax benefits, losses, and liabilities. They'd use terms like total direct expenses incurred, revenues minus direct expense, rate of contribution per unit of revenue, total fixed establishment expenses, and on and on.

I prefer to talk in easily understood terms, rather than ones that accountants take into consideration when calculating your income taxes. Here's what I recommend.

MY PREFERRED BREAK-EVEN FORMULA

Try this formula: *If your monthly mortgage payment is less than or equal to one peak week rental and your property is rented for an average of 17 weeks a year, you will break even financially.*

Here's how this works:

- Your monthly mortgage payment (including taxes and insurance) should roughly be equal to, or less than, the rental income you receive during one peak week. Peak weeks are the highest-earning weeks of the rental season.
- Usually, a vacation rental year has 12 peak weeks. By renting all of these 12 weeks, you'll have enough revenue to pay your mortgage payments for the entire year.
- Other costs, including bills for phone, power, cable, and association dues, are covered by your earnings from approximately five weeks of renting your property during the off-peak season. This means that by renting only 17 weeks out of the year, you can still break even.

Although this formula isn't absolute, it will at least give you a good feel for the numbers. Your property may not fit into this formula. Here are examples of how you can adapt it.

Let's plug in some real numbers and look at this formula as a rent by owner. Remember, if your monthly mortgage payment is equal to or less than one peak week rental rate, then you should be able to achieve positive cash flow. Here's how: Take a property that rents for $1,000 a week during peak season with a monthly mortgage payment of $1,000. There are 12 peak weeks that vary around the country, most if not all of which are generally going to be occupied. If you rent these 12 peak weeks, you have just made enough money to pay one whole year's mortgage payments. Then you'll need to rent five more weeks to pay for incidentals like power, phone, association dues, minor maintenance, and so on. If you have 17 weeks booked (33 percent occupancy), you will have break-even cash flow. Rent more and you'll have positive cash flow.

I base this formula off a 30-year fixed-rate mortgage. I don't necessarily recommend this kind of mortgage, but I use it here because it's the most conservative model. If your property doesn't fit into the formula with a 30-year fixed, consider alternative measures of financing or realize that you may have to take money out of your pocket to offset some of the expenses. For example, your mortgage payment is $2,000 a month and you can rent your place for $1,500 a week. A rough estimate of annual cost for ownership is $34,000 a year ($2,000 × 12 = $24,000 in mortgage payments plus $10,000 in expenses, including phone, furnishings, utilities, cable, HOA dues, insurance, and cost of doing business). That means, optimally, you'd have to rent it for $2,000 a week for 17 weeks. If the property commands only $1,500 a week for 17 weeks to yield $25,500 in revenue, that leaves $8,500 in negative cash flow. For some people, that's acceptable. If this is not acceptable, I suggest you shop for a different kind of loan—an ARM, an interest-only loan, and so on (see Chapter 4). You could lower your payments and make it easier to achieve that break-even cash flow.

PRICING YOUR RENTALS

The subject of pricing anything can be subjective. After all, what's a fair price for an airline ticket? A new car? A steak dinner?

A vacation home rental? The standard answer is, whatever price the rest of the market dictates.

So when it comes to pricing your property for rentals, do what it takes to be "right on the money." When you initially bought your property, you would have learned how much it rented for in that market from your real estate agent. Clearly, the price you advertise directly affects the number of responses you'll get. To determine just the right asking price, research other properties in your area and find out how much other owners are charging for their rentals. The best way to do this is to think and act like a renter. Shop around for rates. Log on to the Internet and start researching. Make sure you're comparing similar properties—apples with apples, not apples with oranges. Also, check with management companies that rent properties in your area. Do whatever it takes to make an informed decision on what you should charge.

It may surprise you to hear this, but you can make a mistake by pricing your property much lower than your competitors. I caution you to be aware of this. While it's certainly acceptable to charge maybe $10 to $50 a week less to give you a competitive edge, pricing a lot lower could give potential renters the wrong impression. It's logical that renters would think your place is inferior to the others under consideration.

When I first started renting by owner, I worried that I'd have to "give away the farm" to attract renters to my properties. Fortunately, fielding a phone call from a renter made me rethink this philosophy. After he saw that my property cost less than others he researched, he asked, "What's wrong with your place?" Shocked, I replied, "What's wrong? Why do you ask?" He responded, "Well, your place is so much cheaper, so there must be something wrong with it!" That really opened my eyes. After that, I raised my price to be exactly the same as the other units in my building and the calls to rent my place flowed in at a steady pace.

Now looking at the opposite end of this issue, what happens if you charge more than comparable rentals in your area? After all, your place might feature granite countertops, expensive furnishings, and other advantages that people could willingly pay more for. If your place is much nicer than the next person's place, you can indeed charge more, especially if you own a single-family dwelling that differs significantly from others in the neighborhood. But if you own a condominium, most likely your unit is laid out exactly like the rest, and therefore people expect to pay about the same amount (unless it's the penthouse). I'd say there's no simple way around it. Yes, your expensive furnishings and fixtures can be used as a selling point. In all likelihood, this means you'll probably book it faster and more often than your competitors' places. But realize that if you charge significantly more than your competitors, then the renters would expect your place to be significantly better.

Different Pricing Structures

Typically, vacation property owners deal with four to eight seasons when it comes to pricing. Generally, these seasons are spring, summer, fall, and winter, plus other "hot" times within those seasons (e.g., spring break or fall foliage times, or when a special sporting event or festival is happening). During these weeks, you'd probably set a higher price than during other times because the demand for rental units is much higher. (See Figure 7.1.)

As you can see from Figure 7.1, the rates for each season have corresponding dates and prices for each time period. First, let's take a look at the corresponding dates. Even though the seasons change in March, June, September, and December, this owner's corresponding dates don't follow the calendar exactly. Often your season will mirror the primary school calendars. Notice that summer rates start in May because for this area May is a month when demand is highest. This could be a property in the South where

FIGURE 7.1 *Seasonal and "Hot" Pricing Structures*

Season	Start	End	Per Night	Per Week	Per Month
Spring	Mar 01	May 25	$185	$925	$ N/A
Spring Break	Mar 23	Apr 20	$ N/A	$1,150	$ N/A
Summer	May 26	Aug 10	$ N/A	$1,350	$ N/A
Late summer	Aug 11	Sep 08	$215	$1,075	$ N/A
Fall	Sep 09	Oct 31	$200	$800	$1,800
Winter	Nov 01	Feb 28	$ N/A	$ N/A	$1,100

Rates do not include 10% Sales Tax and Cleaning Fee.
Pets okay with owner's permission ($25 fee nightly/$150 weekly).
$200 Security Deposit is required.
Note: Until confirmed, rates are subject to change without notice.

children finish their school year in May. By contrast, in the Northeast, peak season might start in late June because that's when school ends in that part of the country.

Naturally, your highest demand will occur during the high or peak season where your property is located. If you own a condo in a ski resort, then winter is your peak season. If you have a vacation home on the beach, then warmer months become peak time. Peak season means you can charge the most amount of money for renting your property.

Notice that some time periods list nightly, weekly, and monthly rates, and some do not. This differentiation is also based on seasonal demand. The owner who advertises "weekly rentals only" obviously won't rent on a nightly basis during the summer. Based on experience, this owner is confident that during the peak season the demand will allow him to rent his place for full weeks. Why would he cut himself short and allow someone to rent for three or four nights when he can have more income from the full-week rental?

On the same note, he doesn't show monthly rates. He could rent for four continuous weeks to one party, but not at a discounted rate for that time period. Again, the demand in high season doesn't require that he discount something he can sell at full price. It's all about thinking like a smart businessperson to maximize your income.

Looking at nightly rates, you can see that the number isn't the weekly rate divided by seven—for good reason. Nightly rates typically are set at one-fifth to one-sixth of the weekly rate. To further entice vacationers to rent, this owner could even advertise a special during his peak season. For example, his ad could say "Rent 5 nights; get 2 nights free," and his options are open for a "Spring special: 33% off regular rates (summer rates)."

In this example, let's take a look at fall rates listed at $200 a night or $800 a week. But, you say, $200 × 5 nights = $1,000, or $200 × 6 nights = $1,200, or $200 × 7 nights = $1,400. Why would he charge only four times one night for a full week? This reduced price is to entice vacationers to stay seven nights. The owner knows that, in his area, there's a high demand for two-night and three-night rentals in the fall so he can charge a higher nightly fee than otherwise. And to encourage vacationers to rent his place for more than two or three nights, he wants to make the weekly charge attractive. I've used this special and have had many "takers." Sometimes they only stay five or six nights, but they still view this as a bargain, and I get more than the otherwise $400 to $600 rental when the place would otherwise be vacant.

Typically, monthly rates are quoted only during the slowest seasons, which in this example, are fall and winter. Generally, monthly rates equal two or three weeks rent during that time period.

A word of caution: Don't get too complicated with your pricing. And be sure to clearly state all extra fees. Notice the footnote below the rates states that sales tax, cleaning fee, pet fee, and security deposit are not included in the rates.

Let every renter know up front all fees that will be assessed. I don't recommend adding the state sales tax figure into your rental price. The sales tax department likes to see taxes listed separately, and besides, the average consumer expects to pay sales tax. (See Appendix C for contact information on state tax offices.)

And don't overlook the last line that states, "Rates are subject to change." Include it for your own protection in case you have old advertising sources milling about. Keep track of every Web site you've ever listed your property on, even all the free sites.

I failed to take my own advice and certainly paid a price. I had listed my rental on a free Web site four years ago. I'd forgotten about it because it didn't produce any inquiries or bookings–until I recently got a call from someone who wanted to rent during a peak week. That caller clearly expected to pay rates that were four years old. What should I do? Honor those rates? Admit my mistake and ask for today's rates at $400 higher? Even though I could fall back on my disclaimer, I acknowledged that rates shouldn't be far away from what's advertised.

In everything I do, I find that honesty is my best policy, so I explained my dilemma to the caller who seemed to understand. We decided on a compromise and split the difference; while I sacrificed $200, the new renters saved $200. But doing this paid off because they did come back. And as you can imagine, I quickly changed my rates on that Web site.

Pet Fees

For owners who accept pets in their vacation rental units (personally, I think it's a good idea because it's a great way to fill your off-season nights as well as make your property more attractive to a larger number of people), it's absolutely appropriate to charge a daily pet fee. Look at it this way: Pet owners know and accept the fact that they have to pay for boarding for their pets whenever they go away. As an owner, I don't want to *encourage* guests to bring their pets (pets can cause damage, but the risk is rarely as great as you imagine). However, if you fail to charge extra for having pets, it could open up the door for a scenario in which renters say something like this: "We want to board Spot because he's such a pain. It would be nice to have a vacation without him, but it's a lot cheaper if we just take him with us."

Still, think of it as a convenience and charge for it, and pet owners will pay willingly. I recommend a pet fee of $10, $20, or $30 a day. In my properties, I charge $25 a night and haven't had any complaints.

Minimum Stays

Many people ask me, should I require a minimum stay? From the example above, you see that it's advantageous to require minimum stays. This owner states a minimum stay of a week in the summer and a month in the winter. In fact, a lot of owners won't rent for fewer than three consecutive nights, with no exception. Others offer nightly rentals all year long. What you decide depends on two things: your preference and what your market dictates. Those who require three-night minimums do this as a quality of life consideration because it's a lot of work to coordinate daily check-ins and checkouts, more checks, more deposits, and more deposits returned for nightly rentals. What is your preference?

June owned a cabin that rented mostly on a nightly basis. She had set up a two-night minimum, then decided to take a leap of faith and changed it to a three-night minimum. As a result, in a year's time, she increased her rental revenue by one-third because she found that, with this rule, people were happy to rent for three nights. Even for those who couldn't stay all three nights, they appreciated being able to stay late into the second day instead of having to check out in the morning. On occasion, she made exceptions to this and rented for two nights, but only as a last resort. In the end, she was pleased that she'd stuck to her guns.

Giving Discounts

Commonly, a prospective renter asks, "Will you give a discount?" My response is sometimes yes and sometimes no, depending on the situation. During peak weeks, for example, I never say yes to discounts. But during months when rentals slow down, be open to negotiation. For example, you could knock off 15 percent for the cleaning fee (but never knock off the sales tax or you could get into trouble with the state collections people). Remember, it's your place so the decision is yours. Keep in mind that each time you allow a renter into your place, you're taking a chance or a risk of liability that something could happen to harm your property. Therefore, some offers just are not worth saying yes to. Someone might want to rent your place for 75 percent off the quoted price. Is it worth it to accept only 25 percent, like a deep discount hotel? What are the possible damages for doing it?

I contend that if you do everything right—you're renting all the weeks during the peak season and achieving positive cash flow—then you need not take that risk. Use your best judgment.

Be careful not to give discounts too early in the booking process. For example, I made it a rule that I wouldn't give a discount until three weeks before the rental date. Learn from the experience of a vacation home owner named Peter.

Peter got a call from a renter 11 months before the rental date. This person wanted to rent Peter's unit during the last two weeks in April and asked if he could receive a discount. Peter looked at his rental records for the past three years and realized he had never rented those two weeks, so he agreed to the discount. He generously gave the caller 30 percent off his normal April rate.

Time passed and in January Peter started getting calls to rent his property for the week of April 19 to 26. He found out that this year Easter was in late April, which created such a high demand that he easily could have rented for full price. The moral of this story is to check the calendar carefully before making special offers!

If you accept credit cards, prospective renters commonly ask, "Will you give a discount for cash payments?" I suggest you answer "yes" but only discount whatever percentage your credit card company charges you. Another caution: Check with your credit card or your merchant account company. It may be against the rules to charge an "up charge" for credit card transactions. If you're going to accept credit cards, just incorporate the cost into your published rates. And give discounts for paying in cash.

Rates for Friends

This question never fails to come up in my seminars: "My friends always ask if they can use my place. What, if anything, should I charge my friends?" Let me preface my answer by saying that the IRS closely scrutinizes the numbers on investment properties that are rented primarily for deeply discounted weeks. IRS analysts pay attention to "investors" who primarily use their properties for family and friends and then declare them as tax shelters. Now, if you're in the business to make money as a vacation home owner, this doesn't pertain to you. But does that mean you shouldn't give discounts to your friends?

Here is how I suggest you handle requests from friends. If they want to stay in your place during a peak week and are willing to book ahead of time, then by all means, let them—and charge full price. If you risk being called stingy or not a true friend, then take this approach and say, "This is an investment and a business. If I give you the week for free, that's like taking $1,350 (the rental rate for the requested week) out of my pocket and handing it right to you. If you'd like to stay at my place for a week and pay less money or go for free, then I'll let you know when I have a last-minute opening. You're welcome to use it when I can't book it."

That may sound cold, but it's the way to run a business. I'm happy to let my friends use my place, but only when it doesn't take money out of my pockets. Or you can always use my old standby, "I'm booked."

You may, of course, want to set a "friends' rate" to cover the cost of using the utilities. I suggest setting a friends' rate at least between $25 and $50 a night. And as a note of caution, don't allow your friends to clean the place themselves before leaving (unless you require all renters to do so). Doing a poor job of cleaning up can be a bad reflection on you if the guests walk into a "less than perfect" place. It could also be a friendship breaker. Instead, insist that they pay the cleaning fee.

Donations, Trades, and Exchanges

Owning a vacation home can offer you wonderful perks, such as the ability to exchange your place for other vacation homes, services, or even tax deductions. For example, if you need repairs, maintenance, or other work done, consider offering the contractor a week at your place instead of paying money.

Indeed, this approach can work well for many types of services that you need at either your vacation or personal home. Just be careful not to shortchange yourself. You could find yourself giving away $1,000 week in exchange for a service that you'd only pay $200 for. Also know that bartered services are subject to taxes, so you must charge and pay sales tax on the bartered cash value.

Trades are fun and easy to do. After all, a major "pitch" for buying a time-share vacation property is that you can trade your "week" and stay at fabulous properties around the world. But did you know you can do exchanges with your vacation investment property, too? Certain Web sites (go to Appendix B) charge a nominal fee for direct and indirect exchanges with owners throughout the world. You might also consider just contacting an owner directly from any of the various sites you find to list or find vacation rentals (see Chapter 9 about hybrid management and advertising). It never hurts to ask.

Also think about donating a week during the slow season as a way to assist a charity or nonprofit group, as well as possibly receiving a tax deduction. (Be sure to speak with your accountant or tax attorney regarding any potential tax deductions. Your deductions depend on the type and terms of the donation, how your business is set up, and how you claim items like donations on your tax return. Therefore, you may or may not be able to deduct this as an advertising expense. In this gray area, have your tax professional determine how it applies to your situation.)

Most charities would be happy to accept your week's donation for an auction or raffle. Again, be sure to write in a clause that the winner must comply with all rental rules and policies. Also be sure to get a damage deposit to cover risks as you normally would.

Ideas and Advice

Become a market watcher and pay close attention to the rates that your competitors charge. Make sure you know about the changing seasons and about rental opportunities during holiday times and special events.

Get creative when it comes to bartering your vacation home for services or other useful purposes. And, most important, never forget that you're running a business. Once you've grasped that concept fully, you'll find that setting rates becomes easier and clearer.

SCREENING GUESTS

Properly screening your guests is your most important duty as an owner. Let me shout this loud and clear: Screen every guest to prevent a disastrous outcome. That means *never accept a booking without speaking to your potential renter on the phone first.* If you insist on skipping this step, then maybe this business isn't right for you. I'm dead serious about that.

Having several e-mail conversations with potential renters might give you a certain level of comfort, but you never know who lurks behind that computer in cyberspace. After all, you've invested too much time and money to give your keys to someone you don't know. You could say, "Well, I don't know them when I talk with them on the phone, either." I disagree. During your telephone conversation, you will indeed get to know them.

Don't worry about having the skill to screen people. Chances are, you've got it; you just don't realize it. Simply be yourself. When speaking with potential renters on the phone, be friendly and personable. Get across the fact that they're renting your second home, and that you care about it. You might also benefit from stressing that you're not a representative of a big management company or impersonal investor, but you're a genuine person just like them.

In support of that, don't perceive the phone-screening process as a dreaded chore. You and the callers aren't planning a funeral; you're planning a vacation, so make it fun. In fact, talking with renters can be highly satisfying, especially when the vacation is followed by compliments and thank-you notes from happy renters.

Don't Discuss Availability at the Start

When screening prospective guests, it's important to use your instincts and be cautious at first. For example, when someone calls, I never say I have anything available until after I've asked some questions. Even if previous e-mail conversations told them my place was available, I could have booked it 15 minutes ago. By keeping the availability in question, you always have an "out" ("Sorry, it's booked") that you can use at any stage of the screening process. When they ask about staying a week, it's better to say, "I think it's open, but I'm not sure. Let me check." Then while I'm "checking," we talk and I get to know them.

Disclosing your availability to renters right from the start could back you into a corner.

Is This Place Right?

First thing I ask is how many adults *and* how many children. I may even ask the ages of their children. As I engage them in conversation, I learn a lot about the family because people usually like to share all sorts of information about themselves. You may find yourself doing the same.

As if I were a travel agent matching the renters' needs with the property, I make sure that my property is truly the right place for them. For example, if they want a place in the hustle and bustle of town and my place is secluded, I advise them to continue searching.

What? Turn down a potential renter? Sure. And here's what I ask myself: Do I want people staying at my place if they won't be happy there? Do I want them to curse me when they find out it's not what they expected? Think about possible ramifications for yourself. If renters aren't happy, will they take care of your place? Will they call and demand a refund? Will they take a complaint to the extreme and sue you for false advertising? Best not to go there! I say, just be honest.

Yes, I have tried to talk many people *out of* renting my place. Some choose to rent it anyway, but at least I've told them what they are getting into. If you do that too, they will respect you (and your property) even more.

Do Detective Work First

Consider doing preliminary screening work before even speaking to a potential renter on the phone. When you receive e-mail inquiries, for example, do some detective work. Look for clues in their e-mail addresses. If an address is big-bad-boy@college.edu, what's your first clue? Big Bad Boy, possibly. Even the college.edu can be a clue.

However, I'd still reply to this e-mail as I do every other, because this inquiry could be coming from a professor or a university employee or even the daughter or son doing research for parents. Don't rule out potential renters solely because of their e-mail addresses; still, keep your antenna up during your screening phone call.

Families Make Good Renters

In my experience, families with small children make the best renters. Now, some people believe little ones can be worse than renting to college kids. But don't be concerned about them scribbling crayon on the walls or spilling grape juice on the rugs because this rarely happens. If you decline renting to families, realize that your risk of "not renting" increases substantially. You'd not only be cutting yourself off from at least 50 percent of your prospective renters but, riskier than that, you could be violating the law. Yes, you are allowed to set age restrictions, *but* you can't discriminate against families with children under 18 unless your property is located in a community that has licensing exclusions to do so (such as 55+ adult communities). Another exception would be if the home poses a danger to children. For example, you own a vacation home in a historic district of a town, and it has been designated a historic building. That means certain elements of the house can't be altered—perhaps it's the original lead paint or the old railings. Since you can't bring these up to code, the building therefore poses a danger to children, so you can't accept them.

However, if your place doesn't fall into that category and you clearly don't want to allow kids, don't state that in your advertising. You could open yourself up to a discrimination suit.

Over-25 Adults Only

When I ask, "How many adults and how many children?" my antennae go up if the answer is "all adults." That's when I adopt a different mind-set or use my "out" ("Sorry, I'm booked"). I don't often play that card right away—as in any game, it's best to hold onto your last-resort options until the end. Naturally, I don't want to rule out *all* people with no children; I only want to rule out those adults who are under 25.

To find out their ages, simply ask. Believe it or not, most will answer honestly. You'll find that if they're 25 or older, most often they'll feel flattered by your questions and tell you about themselves. Simply make it easy to engage in conversation and get to know them. And if they are indeed under 25, it may be a good time to use your "out."

What if you ask their ages and they lie? Sure, you could require proof such as a copy of their driver's license, but come on. If they lie over the phone, chances are great that they'll lie in writing, too. Teenagers get fake IDs. Having copies of those fake IDs would only provide you with a false sense of security because you'd have to verify that the IDs they send are really theirs.

Instead, when speaking with them and you sense from their voices or demeanor that they're under 25, you can use your "out" at this point. Before you do, consider employing a tactic like this: "Well, I just have to ask and make sure that you are really over 25. Because, you see, I am not allowed to rent to anyone under 25. It's not *my* rule; it's the association's rule. Our home is in an association and the bylaws state that we are not allowed to rent to anyone under 25. They're strict about it, too. If the association finds out, they will evict you and I have absolutely no say in the matter. And if you get evicted, then you lose all your rent money and your deposit."

That usually scares them off. If it doesn't, you still have your last "out"—"Sorry, it's booked!"

Pros and Cons of Setting Restrictions

While it's acceptable to have any policies and restrictions you want (within the law), please realize that the more restrictive you are, the fewer renters you'll attract. For some owners that may be fine, but to have maximum occupancy, learn the importance of flexibility.

For example, you may want to consider an exception to the under-25 rule. You may have a tough time finding renters who are 25 or over in ski resort towns. After all, many skiers and snowboarders are college students. And plenty of responsible college kids are around. But to cover yourself, ask for a large deposit, require a midweek cleaning at an extra charge (so the cleaning person can assess any problems while cleaning the place), and make it clear that you will not tolerate any hell-raising. Make it clear that if you get a call from neighbors or from the police, they will be evicted and have to forfeit their deposit. Don't just say this; write it specifically into the rules.

Allowing Pets

Remember that for every group of people you exclude, you write off the possibility of renting to a large pool of potentially good guests, including pet owners. Indeed, some pet owners won't leave home without their dogs and only look for vacation homes that will allow them to take Fido along for the trip. And here's a little secret. If people have a dog that travels with them, chances are excellent that *this* dog won't cause problems or they'd keep him at home! Assume that they want a relaxing vacation and so would only bring along dogs who are well behaved.

Just allowing pets can dramatically increase your occupancy and your revenue from 10 to 50 percent! Charge an additional $10 to $30 a night, or $70 to $210 a week, and use that money for extra cleaning. If you rent out six to eight weeks, the increased revenue could be enough to totally replace a carpet.

Pets can be a big factor in attracting off-season rentals. One of my properties is always booked for spring and summer but rarely had fall bookings. This three-bedroom unit is ideal for families. When kids are in school, couples without kids look to rent vacation homes. However, they look for one-bedroom places. So when I decided to accept pets in the fall only, these couples started booking, and I was able to stay booked for all of September and October. Needless to say, that policy will stay in place.

An owner named Jennifer has a nice cabin in the mountains of Colorado. Although it was within driving distance of three ski resorts, it wasn't close enough to advertise that her place was associated with any of them. Jennifer was only booking her cabin two or three weeks a year, but the minute she added that she'd accept pets, more bookings started to flow in. Two years after making this change, her cabin is booked to skiers for the whole ski season and 3 or 4 weeks during the summer to hikers, plus 10 to 12 long weekends through the year. She said that she has to clean the carpet more often, but it has been well worth it, and she has now bought the cabin right next door, too.

Wheelchair and Handicap Accessibility

Making your property wheelchair and handicap accessible can bring in more renters at little or no additional risk. People (and they're not only older people) who have handicaps and use wheelchairs have a hard time finding accessible vacation properties to rent. Often they have to stay in hotels simply because they have no other choices. If you can buy an accessible property, do so. Or consider upgrading your place to make it accessible. You might be surprised to find that sometimes it costs very little to upgrade. However, be sure to refer to government guidelines when upgrading your property or advertising it as such. For example, to make a property wheelchair accessible, guidelines require you to have 36-inch doorways, a roll-in shower, assistance bars in the bathroom, an elevator, and so on.

Note there are different types of special needs accessibility; for example, someone who uses a walker has different needs than someone who uses a wheelchair. A visually impaired person also has a different set of needs. Be sure to carefully check out these requirements before making any structural changes. Do your homework.

Value-Added Items

What can you add to your property that will increase its occupancy? To answer that question, think about the group that represents the largest percentage of renters—families with children. I can't tell you how many times people have called and said my property didn't quite match what they wanted, but they booked it anyway because it has a high chair and portable crib. Availability of the high chair and porta-crib *sold* the booking. Those two things only cost about $150 and can pay you back 100 times over. Plus, consider things that kids like: toys, games, videos, bikes—the list is endless.

Study your marketplace to determine what other things add value. For example, if your place is in Colorado, don't even consider renting it without a hot tub. In Minnesota, a sauna is a must. Vacationers in Las Vegas want a private pool. Renters in Gatlinburg demand a pool table. Although you might regard these as pricey additions, they often pay for themselves with the number of extra bookings you'll get.

Also, remember that a sofa bed or futon can sleep two more people, which can very well be the difference between renting out your place or not.

Last-Minute Renters

Don't rule out last-minute renters in your strategy. Although your goal should be to avoid such bookings (they make your life too complicated and it's easier to have them booked well in advance), it may not always be possible. Make an exception to your rule. For example, you could post last-minute specials on many of the Web sites where you advertise. A better strategy is to change the quick description line you have created—the one that pops up every time renters search for vacation rentals using the portal sites (which bring them to a listing of properties in your area, including yours). If your original description is "Great 3 BR condo on the beach," change it to "3 BR on beach, last-minute cancellation OPEN 11/19-11/30." There's an excellent chance that one little change will make your phone ring.

No Need for a Hard Sell

Finding good renters isn't that hard overall. So when you get inquiries, don't feel obliged to "hard sell" anyone (after all, they called you, not the other way around). In your conversation with potential renters, if you find out about a drawback or hesitation (e.g., they want a view of the beach and your place is a block away), find ways to turn that to your advantage.

Cindy owns a home near the beach but not exactly on the beach, and it doesn't have a good beach view. Every caller tends to ask this question first: "What kind of view do you have?" Cindy used to say, "Sorry, I have no view" and the renters would close the conversation. Then she considered two ways to get around it. Her first option was to sell her place and buy another on the beach. But properties on the beach cost $100,000 more on average than those a block away. She simply couldn't afford to pay the extra $100,000 so she abandoned that idea. Her second option made a lot more sense. She diligently searched the Internet for nearby properties on the ocean with a good view. She found out that they not only cost more to buy, but they also cost more to rent. Here's how she now answers that first key question (and gets more bookings because of it):

Renter: "Do you have a view?"

Cindy: "Sorry, when we bought the place, I really wanted that view too, but we just couldn't afford it. Then I asked myself, how much time am I really going to spend in the place anyway? I'll be on the beach every day. So we bought this place and I love it."

Renter: "Sorry, I really wanted the view."

Cindy: "That's okay, I understand. Let me see. I do know of some other owners who have properties with a great view. Okay, here's the same type unit as mine, two bedrooms, two baths, great view. Do you want their name and number?"

Renter: "Sure, please!"

Cindy: "Okay, it's # 24AB5 on VRBO.com, John Smith, phone number 234-123-4567. . . wow, his place is really nice; nice price, too."

Renter: "Really? How much?"

Cindy: "Well, it's $800 more per week than mine, but it's nice."

Renter: "Oh, I really can't afford that. Can you tell me more about your place? Maybe it wouldn't be so bad not to have the view . . ."

Cindy isn't pushing something the renter doesn't want; remember, the renter contacted her first. In your conversations, you'll discover that, at first, renters want everything: the view, the large size, the location, the most for their money, and more. But when they narrow it down, they realize they can compromise. You simply help them decide which compromises to make.

Think Strategically

Finding ideal renters involves much more than screening out the few potential bad apples. Be creative and think strategically about all those people who might make great renters, if only you give them a chance.

Yes, by all means, use discretion and don't just rent to every person who comes your way. But don't be close-minded either. Consistently practicing the screening process makes you savvier with your "people detector" skills. You'll learn to identify people you can trust and those you can't. And don't be afraid to make exceptions to your general rules whenever you deem it wise. This story drives home my point perfectly.

The first year I owned my property in Destin, Florida, I worried about whether I would ever get renters. One of my first calls came from a mother looking for a place where her teenage daughter and four of her friends could go on a trip as a senior getaway. "Is Mom coming too?" I asked. "Nope." Of course, my initial reaction was "No way!"

Then I chatted with the mom and explained my policies. She offered a huge deposit and reassured me that these girls were well-behaved young adults who didn't drink or smoke. This mother seemed so genuine (plus I'm a sucker for a good story) that I let the girls rent my place and everything went well. I had no regrets about following my instincts in this situation.

Six years later, I got a phone call from this same mom. She said that her daughter had now graduated from college and was getting married (she was still under 25) and loved our place so much that she wanted to spend her honeymoon there. Naturally, I said yes. I can't tell you how good that made me feel about my decision in that first year.

It's indeed okay to use your heart when screening potential guests. And who knows, you may just be securing potential renters for years to come.

HOW TO HANDLE KEYS FOR RENTERS

You live in Indiana, your renters live in Texas, and your property is in Colorado. How do you get keys to renters? Don't worry, this doesn't have to be as complicated as it seems.

You have many options when it comes to keys. First, you can use the old-fashioned method of mailing the keys to your renters. Many owners have been doing this for 20 or even 30 years or more. Early in our marriage, my husband and I vacationed on Martha's Vineyard every year. We rented directly from an owner. She would mail us the keys before we left, and we would mail them back after we returned. It was effective. Effective, but not necessarily simple.

You may not have given it much thought, but mailing keys leaves a lot of room for error. And it means more work than is really necessary. The problem is you have to make numerous sets of keys, send them out in a timely manner so that your renters receive them before they leave home, and be sure they mail the keys back to you. Forget any one of these steps and you will have a potentially serious problem on your hands. What if the renters forget to bring the keys with them when they leave home? What if they don't send them back? What if they lose them while staying there?

I think the best way to alleviate all this trouble is to drop the idea of mailing keys and go with your second option: Buy a simple combination lockbox. A lockbox attaches to your doorknob or somewhere on your property. The most common ones (made by GE) are inexpensive ($25 to $30) and can be found at hardware stores, locksmith stores, or on the Internet.

A lockbox isn't a complex piece of equipment. You can easily set your own code, hang it on your doorknob, and put the keys into it. You then give renters the combination to the box when you send them driving directions. (They usually don't forget the directions when they leave home, and even if they do, you could always give them the code over the phone.) The downside is that you can't change the code on this type of lockbox after each group of renters.

Your third option is to buy a keyless entry door lock. Similar to what you see in most banks and offices, it has pushbuttons right on the locks. These locks are great but can be expensive at $200 to $600 each. They also can be found online or through most locksmiths and hardware stores.

You also might consider the newest type of electronic keyless lock, the kind that offers remote access. Again, they're quite pricey but do offer the convenience of being able to store, change, and create combinations right from your home computer or even via cell phone. The downside (besides price) is that most work on batteries. Anything electronic can malfunction, and the batteries, although they usually last three years, can go dead. These types of locks also have a monthly service fee associated with them.

So why tell you about them? Because for many owners, this may be the only option they have (aside from mailing keys). In fact, many condominium complexes prohibit lockboxes. In some, even real estate agents aren't allowed to use them. (These complexes most likely have an on-site rental management company. I doubt that these companies will hand out your keys to your guests because now you're a competitor!)

Lost Keys

Okay. You get the phone call, the inevitable one you knew would come one of these days. Your upset renter says they went to the beach, a big wave hit, and the keys got lost (or some variation of that).

What do you do if your renters lose the keys to your place? Well, if you decide to purchase one of the keyless locks, this won't be a problem for you. But if you use either of the other two methods, then this will likely happen eventually.

The best way to prevent this is by setting up a plan ahead of time. The most logical solution is to get a replacement key from your housekeeper. (See, I told you housekeepers are your lifelines!) Be proactive in setting up the arrangements. Would your housekeepers want your renters to call directly or should you have them call you first? If they have to come out, how much would they charge? I suggest setting up a different fee for regular business hours than for after-hours or in the middle of the night. When you've decided on fees, be sure to state them on your rental rules. (See Appendix A for sample Rules and Regulations.)

Ahh, you're now thinking, if they have locked themselves out but your phone number and the housekeeper's number are inside the condo, how can they call? As a crafty owner, I have thought of every angle. (Actually, I got burned once and I learned from my mistake.) Here's the simple solution: Put a sticker inside the lockbox with your contact numbers on it. This way, because the lockbox always stays on the door, they can open it and retrieve this information.

In addition, you can distribute keys to people you trust who might be able to help in this situation. That way, if your housekeeper is unavailable, your renters' needs are still covered. For example, give keys to other owners, association managers, maybe even the agent who sold you the place. And you want to make friends with your neighbors anyway! (See Chapter 12, "Being a Good Neighbor (from Afar).")

Now, the next solution is to hide a key somewhere. In a single-family dwelling, that's easy to do. You can even purchase a second key box, put a different code on it, and mount it in an obscure place (this is good for maintenance people, too, because you'd be giving a different code than your lockbox code used by renters). If you own a condominium, you'll have to be more creative.

After my first incident when my guests got locked out, I got very inventive. Here's what happened.

It was Fourth of July weekend. I was in upstate New York and my cell phone rang. It was my housekeeper in Florida. She had had an accident and was in the hospital (thankfully not badly injured). But she wouldn't be able to clean my condo. And, of course, I had guests due to arrive in just a few hours. My first thought was "Oh no," but then I remembered that I'm a proactive owner! I have a backup cleaning person. When I called her, she just happened to be at the unit downstairs. No problem, she agreed to clean my place, too. I hung up and thought, "Good. Solved." But an hour later, she called to tell me her key didn't fit my door. My blood pressure shot through the ceiling! I forgot to give her a key the last time I changed the locks. But again, I had a solution. "No problem, here's my lockbox code," I said. "The keys are inside." She called back two minutes later. "Christine, I got the lockbox open and there are no keys inside." My blood pressure must have soared off the chart. My last renters either forgot to put the keys inside the lockbox or *they left them inside. Now what? I thought and thought, then–an epiphany! I gave her the lockbox code to another owner's property upstairs. I told her to go inside to the utility closet and feel the backside of the hot water tank (I'm sure she thought I was nuts!). Taped there was a key! That one I did remember to replace when I last changed the locks. Using that key, she was able to go and clean my place before the next guests arrived. Disaster averted.*

Liability with Keys

How do you deal with the liability associated with keys? First and foremost, be sure that whoever you give your keys to is trustworthy. Do *not* put the address or unit number on any key, especially hidden keys. Also, be sure to explain in writing (on the directions is fine) that the code is not changed after each checkout, so your renters will have that information. Also, tell them not to use the lockbox as a holding spot for the keys while they're out.

As an owner, I suggest you install some type of keyless lock on the inside of the property in addition to your regular lock. This increases the safety factor for the people inside. The lock can either be an old-fashioned chain or a keyless dead bolt. You certainly wouldn't want anyone to be able to use a key to get inside and harm your guests.

Like so many issues associated with vacation home rentals, the important thing to remember is that a little planning goes a long way toward avoiding future problems. Just think of how I solved the key dilemma for my Florida property while I was in New York. The only reason this story had a happy ending was because I'd built what NASA would call "redundancy" into my system. When they send a spacecraft millions of miles away from Earth, what if something goes wrong? NASA builds backup systems that cover equipment that fails. Think about keys in the same way. After all, though you're not millions of miles away, you may well be *hundreds* of miles away—bad enough. Of course, a backup system for keys is much easier than fixing a probe sent into deep space, and you don't need to be a rocket scientist to do it.

BENEFITS OF RENTING BY OWNER

It's easier than you think to overcome doubts and hesitations you may have about renting out your property yourself. Beyond the ability to keep more money because you're not paying a management company's commissions, you'll reap many additional benefits.

Of these benefits—possibly even more important than profits—is that renting out your property yourself is the best insurance against damages. You get to control who rents your vacation home, which becomes an informal brand of "damage insurance." I always talk to each renter before making any arrangements. I'm friendly and personable, and let prospective guests know that they are renting my second home. By establishing a good relationship early on, I find that they transform from "customer" to "friend." Compare that to the experience of staying in a hotel. If you spill coffee on the hotel room carpet, what do you do? You leave it. But if you rent a "friend's" place, how differently would you handle that spilled coffee? In my experience, my renters make the effort to take care of such issues—just like a friend would.

Similar to staying in a hotel, the experience of renting from a management company is quite often impersonal. Most people don't even know that the properties are individually owned; they think they're owned by the management company. But when renters form a bond with you and get the feeling that you really care about your place, they will, too. After all, they are guests in your home.

8

WORKING WITH A PROPERTY MANAGEMENT COMPANY

In Chapter 7, you read about how to manage your vacation home rental business on your own. It's also the subject of my first book, *How to Rent by Owner: The Complete Guide to Buy, Manage, Furnish, Rent, Maintain and Advertise Your Vacation Rental Investment* (go to http://www.HowToRentByOwner.com for details). Let me make a disclaimer here and say I am a rent-by-owner advocate and can't change the color of my coat. I think management companies charge too much money. However, I can appreciate circumstances and preferences that make working with a property management company the best choice for you.

BREAK-EVEN FORMULA USING A MANAGEMENT COMPANY

Now, let's look at our break-even formula when using a management company. For the sake of argument, let's just say you rent the same number of weeks, 12 peak and 5 other weeks, and your rental rate is the same. For every week you rent, management companies take 30 percent for commissions (usually more, but I'll be conservative). So now your $1,000 becomes $700. Then the management company charges you a cleaning fee of $50 ("by owners" charge the renter). Now your $700 becomes $650. If your renters use a credit card, you get charged a 2 percent fee. American Express is even more. So your $650 becomes $630. With these charges alone, you have just given away 37 percent of your money. Therefore, you would need to book 27 weeks (52 percent occupancy) to equal the same amount of net cash in your pocket as the person who rents by owner. What I'm saying here is that you will need to rent 10 more weeks with a management company to come up with the same money. Math doesn't lie.

Truly, the example above is a very conservative figure. If you currently use a management company, you are probably shaking your head and saying, "No way." Besides the commissions, add the other incidental charges and fees, then you'll see that the figure that the management companies keep becomes more like 50 to 60 percent of your gross profit.

This chapter discusses how to find and work with companies that act on your behalf when renting out your vacation home.

Susan's greatest doubt was whether she could manage her own property from 500 miles away. How could she possibly deal with problems quickly enough from such a distance? She decided to hire a property manager to increase her comfort level and so she could get "up and running" with her new venture right away. In her first year of vacation property ownership, she appreciated having this security blanket–the cushion between her and her renter to deal with the hassles–and learned what to expect month to month as a new owner.

FINDING A PROPERTY MANAGEMENT COMPANY

When researching a management company to work with, start by analyzing the results that come up on search engines through the Internet. The number one objective for the management company that you choose is "Can the company rent your property?" Property management companies that are "with it" focus on building their Internet presence, which is the number one place vacationers look for properties.

Look to see where the company comes up on a search engine by putting in the name of the town and the key words "vacation rental." If you see the particular company's name come up again and again, that's certainly a company you want to investigate. You have the evidence that it spent time, effort, and money to achieve good advertising through a high Internet ranking. In addition to Internet research, ask your real estate agent for names of management companies that manage vacation properties similar to yours. Agents can steer you away from the known "bad apples" in the community. Also they constantly visit properties so they can see if the management companies are doing a good job of maintaining them. Agents can be an excellent source of referrals.

So can people who own properties in the area. Says Erin, who worked with a management company in Gatlinburg, "You're doing yourself a disservice if you don't talk with other owners." She suggests that when looking for a management company, talk with different people about various companies and get a wide perspective on services and pricing. Buyer beware: The least expensive option isn't always the best. For example, one company can charge a lower-than-average commission rate but may have fees in other areas that make up for it. "The place I went with charged me a 30 percent commission but also charged 8 percent for credit card fees and had fees for firewood, hot tub maintenance, cleaning, and so on. Other companies' commission rates included the cleaning and some other charges."

Some companies like to give away free nights to travel agents and often write that in the contract with the property owner. Others spell out the commission rate and procedures if the owner books a rental or if a travel agent books it. (Generally, the management company would pay the owner or travel agent 10 percent for that booking.)

On-site versus Off-site

Many condominium complexes have on-site management. Some have exclusive management company contracts, meaning if you rent out your vacation home through a property manager, you must use their on-site company.

Jeff bought in a well-established complex. He didn't warm up to people in the on-site management company, so he signed on with a different one. But since the on-site company had managed the properties for 30 years, most of the guests knew to go to its offices. He realized he was missing out on a lot of rentals.

On the flip side, Barbara went to a new on-site management company that just started dealing with owners and renters in a new complex. This management company had a difficult time renting the properties because it hadn't yet become established in the community.

Some complexes have exclusive on-site management companies but allow renting by owner. However, sometimes the management company owns or controls the amenities and won't allow the vacationers who are renting by owner to use the amenities, even on a fee basis. For example, Simone chooses to rent her property by owner, but her renters can't use the fitness center, childcare center, or other amenities. That forces her to be up front communicating with her renters about this policy.

DO YOUR HOMEWORK

Always think of yourself as an astute consumer and check around. Do your homework extremely well when selecting a management company. Since there is no governing body overseeing management companies as in other industries, due diligence is extremely important. You can start by contacting the Better Business Bureau in the community where the company is located and find out if any complaints have been reported.

I can't emphasize doing as much homework as possible. Keep in mind that you are handing over the management of your second home, which is probably worth $200,000 to $500,000. I believe it's imperative to learn about the company's reputation and determine its trustworthiness before signing any agreements. A lot of people won't let close friends drive their cars, yet unbelievably they turn over their half-million-dollar properties to unknown companies.

Use these ideas and questions to learn about the processes and credibility of every management company you consider working with.

Questions to Ask Management Companies

- Do you give owners copies of every vacationer's statement? (You have a right to have these.) Please show me a past statement for a property similar to mine. (If they're concerned about confidentiality, ask them to block out that information on the photocopy you receive.)
- What is the revenue split you provide owners (e.g., 60/40, 70/30, and so on)? If I get a booking myself, then what is the revenue split?
- How do you advertise the properties? Which avenues bring in the most qualified inquiries?

- Do you collect, pay, and file the state sales tax on my behalf?
- What are the expected costs for advertising, marketing, cleaning, maintenance, etc.? Typically, what other costs are owners responsible for?
- What expenses do you ask renters to cover?
- Is there a maximum amount that the company is authorized to approve for maintenance issues without getting the owner's preapproval?
- What is not covered under the commission split? Is there a cap on the extras you charge for?
- What is your procedure for collecting and returning security deposits?
- What are the contractual agreements you use?
- What are the penalties if I choose to back out of my contractual agreement with you?
- Under the agreement, when can I use the property myself? Is there a limit to the number of owner weeks I can have? (Knowing this helps you determine if you're giving the company exclusive rights to rent your property. It's also a factor when it comes to paying income tax. Please see Chapter 4 for details.)
- Please give me the names and contact information of owners you work with now and owners you've worked with in the past.

Questions to Ask Property Owners

Next, call the owners referred by the management company and others, and ask:

- How frequently did this company rent out your property?
- How well does the company's advertising work, in your opinion?

- Are you happy with the service you're receiving? Can you give examples of times when the company has given you both good and bad service?
- If you've ever had damages to your place, how did the company respond to fixing them?
- How well do people in this company communicate with you?
- Do they pay your portion of the rental income in a timely manner? What day of the month do you see that money come in?
- How much do you pay for extra maintenance on your place above the standard amount that's been quoted?
- Do you know other owners who once used this company and stopped? If so, why did they discontinue the relationship? Can you give me contact information so I can ask them direct questions?
- What regular maintenance details are scheduled? How well does the management company handle them? (For example, while one owner was staying in her place, she shampooed the carpets and told the management company that task was done. However, the next week, the carpets were shampooed again as part of the regular maintenance. She was billed for the cleaning.)
- How does the management company work with the homeowners association?
- How were your renters treated by the management company? Please share specific experiences you can think of.
- What were the exact charges your renters had to pay? When you compared the charges the renters were charged with those you received, did you find any discrepancies? (For example, unethical companies have been known to charge a cleaning fee to both the owner and the vacationer.)

HOW TO WORK WITH YOUR MANAGEMENT COMPANY

Property management companies take a commission of 20 to 40 percent of the rental revenue to manage a property. They're responsible for facilitating booking, advertising, marketing, cleaning, and maintenance, but in most cases, that 20 to 40 percent covers only the booking fee. You're still financially responsible for every aspect of cleaning and maintaining your property in addition to paying the mortgage and other expenses (e.g., utilities, maintenance, Web site expenses, etc.). Get a list of *all* fees in writing. A lot of misunderstanding can take place regarding who pays for what, so clarify each of your respective responsibilities in the early stages of discussion.

Creating Good Relationships

Here are some tips for creating good relationships with your management company:

- Make it clear that your number one priority is to have open channels of communication, that you expect issues to be dealt with in a reasonable amount of time.
- Determine the best way to communicate with people in the management office. When is it best to use e-mail? When is it best to call on the phone?
- Spell out your expectations about how soon you need to hear back from them on a specific issue. If it requires immediate attention that could affect the ability to rent your property, ask for a response within 24 hours. If you haven't heard back in that time frame, it's reasonable to call them again and remind them what needs to be done. If the issue isn't urgent—"My son left a toy behind so please put it in the

owner's closet."—then don't put pressure on them to get it done immediately.

- When you have an urgent situation such as a leaky faucet, broken heater or air conditioner, or malfunctioning major appliance, expect the company to give you a plan of action and time line when repairs will take place. Don't accept excuses like the maintenance man is sick; demand the company solve every little problem before it develops into a big one.

- If you haven't had a booking from your management company lately, you don't want to be a pest but you do want to know what's happening. Don't put people on the pointed end of the stick with a harsh phone call. Rather, send a diplomatically written e-mail and ask for someone to follow up within three or four days. Again, give them clear expectations about what you want and when you need to hear back from them.

- Those people who make reservations can make a big difference. Treat them very well; they're your first line of communication with their customers who are ultimately your customers, too.

- Be pleasant. If you call and sound like a whiny, complaining, grouchy owner, you're not making friends and risk ruining a good relationship. Who will they think of when a booking opportunity comes in—nice Erin or grumpy George?

- Don't call every day and take away time from doing what you've hired the company to do.

- Choose your battles wisely. If you have an issue that affects booking or maintenance, definitely call. But if you're questioning what's happening or being chatty, that's not a good use of time.

- Keep the company posted on improvements you're making to your property. Let them know about upgrades, like adding a new stereo in the bedroom. These communications show you care about your property and makes their job of "selling" it easier. (Some owners make no improvements over the years yet expect the reservationists to put them on an equal footing with active owners.)

- Not everyone responds quickly by e-mail so take that into consideration. But make sure to convey that you consider all forms of communication to be urgent. After all, this is a business arrangement.

Talking with Renters Directly

When is it okay to pick up your phone and talk to your renters directly? Some owners like to get feedback on their experience and ask: "Was the place in good shape? How well were you treated by the management company?" Others feel they are being nosy and could make company representatives nervous. When they rent through a management company, guests generally perceive that owners are hands-off, so they might be suspicious if they get a fact-finding phone call.

If you think a call would make the renters feel uncomfortable, putting them in the position of tattling on the management company, you've accomplished nothing. On the other hand, if you have a reason to call (for example, the hot tub had been malfunctioning), don't hesitate to call and say, "I don't want to interrupt your vacation time, but I want to make sure the hot tub repairs are complete." With that call, the renters get the message that you care about your place, and they'll take greater care of it themselves.

Calling them can certainly personalize their rental experience and create a personal connection. To them, the difference between renting from a person and renting from a storefront (management company) is like night and day. People don't admit they broke dishes or damaged something to the management company because they're afraid they'll have to pay extra fees. They tend to see the property manager as an impersonal corporate "owner," so when something goes wrong, they are less open about telling the management company than they would be an owner.

PROS AND CONS OF HIRING A MANAGEMENT COMPANY

Many investors buy vacation homes strictly for the appreciation they'll realize over time (see Chapter 10). They're often busy professionals who live far away from their second homes and have no interest in fielding calls for bookings or maintenance issues. They appreciate the convenience of working with a management company but always feel a need to be less than trusting.

The Terry family in California had owned a condo on the Hawaiian island of Kauai for some time. They contracted with a management company on-site to rent their condo, but reports kept coming back that no rentals had come in. However, their neighbors in California rented a nearby condo for two weeks and watched people come and go from the Terry condo the whole time. Again that month, the management company reported no rental activity during that period. The Terrys questioned the manager's integrity and quit working with the company. Unfortunately, they had no way to find out how much potential income they'd lost.

When renting from afar, you take a risk that you're not working with trustworthy people. How do you know when vacationers rent your place? To provide electronic spying, some owners have turned to installing an electronic lock that records when anyone goes in and out of their place. It costs $600 to $1,000 and can be monitored through the Internet.

Still, dreams of having mutually beneficial relationships can go south, as Natalie's story tells.

Before we got married in 1998, my husband and I purchased nine acres of land in a vacation area of Tennessee. Until my husband died in 2003, we built eight cabins for overnight rentals, plus one to live in. Over those years, we worked almost exclusively with rental companies to book our cabins with vacationers. Our first company nickeled-and-dimed us to death, so we switched to a small family-owned company that seemed to be doing a booming business. Because my husband agreed to do the maintenance work, this company agreed to set up an 80/20 split on the percentage of money received (a 60/40 split is customary). For the first three months our cabins rented almost every night. But we didn't get any money from this company. Before long, it owed us $23,000, which I'll likely never see. We cut off the company as our managers as soon as it became clear we wouldn't get paid. In fact, by reading the local papers, I learned that all its properties went into foreclosure. We hired an attorney who found out that the owners split up. After taking legal action, I managed to have the wife's wages garnished, but I only received $3,000 of the $23,000 owed us.

After that fiasco, we signed with another management company. These people did only a fair job of booking rentals, probably because they weren't aggressive with their Internet advertising. Naturally we wondered why this company couldn't do well attracting renters. We did appreciate the honest way it did business; it just didn't bring in enough renters for us.

About the time my husband passed away, I hired yet another rental company, plus I started renting the cabins myself. I did my best to coordinate all the bookings and still maintain the cabins, too. Hanging over my head was the fact that I had to pay a high mortgage note every month. It was a tough time; I got so stressed and overwhelmed running the rental business, I didn't even have time to grieve over the loss of my husband.

In the beginning of 2004, I decided to turn the cabin rentals over to yet another management company. The people there didn't pay me, and in effect forced me out of business with their dishonest tactics.

Our dream turned into a nightmare. I ended up having to hire a lot of maintenance help and couldn't make any money, even running the business myself. I had to work through the process, emotionally and financially, of renting the properties. My husband thought the cabins would set me up for life. But I knew I wasn't making as much money as I should have. And I knew I couldn't do this for the next 20 years.

I finally realized I had to get out and sold my rental cabins. In the final analysis, I asked myself, "Was this a good investment?" I had to answer "Yes"–from a financial point of view anyway. Based on what my husband paid for the cabins and what I sold them for, the return ended up being much greater than putting that money into the stock market.

The most important lessons I learned were to find ethical management companies to work with and to plan for what could go wrong.

SWITCHING MANAGEMENT COMPANIES

If you're unhappy with your current company, you'll likely find alternative companies that better suit your needs. When you're ready to take the plunge and switch companies, ask your new company how it recommends you handle the transition.

In addition to asking the questions listed earlier in this chapter, ask:

- What is the best timing to make the switch?
- Should I wait until you have reservations on the books before I give the other company notice? If so, how long?
- What if the other company wants to drop my bookings? How can you help me prevent that from happening?

Saying Good-bye to Your Management Company

What should you do if you already have a management company, but you've decided you want to discontinue the arrangement? When is the best time to fire your management company?

Definitely, I don't recommend ending a contract with your management company in the middle of the peak rental season, because most vacationers have already booked their accommodations. (Most bookings are made 60 to 90 days before the peak season.) While you get through the current peak season, simultaneously advertise and book guests for the future so you can have a smooth transition into self-management before next year's peak rental season. You're now truly in business for yourself as you learn to manage your rental business by owner from a distance (see Chapter 7).

Contractual Agreements

What if your situation goes south in a hurry, but you've got a 12-month contract? At the beginning of the contractual agreement, you could negotiate for a shorter term so you can try out the company and determine if it's a good fit. If the people running the company are worth their salt, they'll have no fear of signing a shorter contract. Remember, it's in your best interest to make sure the contract suits your needs. If you feel uncomfortable signing the proposed contract or believe the company isn't keeping up its side of the deal, consult your attorney for advice.

Erin had a good relationship with her management company and they communicated well. She had signed a one-year contract but decided to "fly" on her own after the contract expired. She continued on a month-to-month basis for four months afterward to honor the bookings the company had made. She wanted to keep those bookings rather than have them go to other properties managed by the same company.

As an alternative to leaving completely, you could discuss setting up a partnership or hybrid program with your management company.

PARTNERSHIP ARRANGEMENTS

Setting up a partnership program combines your doing some of the rental work and a management company doing some. Your aim is to find a compromise—a balance—between hiring a management company and doing all of the work yourself by setting up a partnership program.

How do you find out about these programs? Some management companies openly offer them. But if yours doesn't, I suggest you create one to suit yourself, following ideas you read about in this chapter and elsewhere. Certainly ask other owners to learn what they're doing. I encourage you to go directly to the management company and offer its decision makers a deal. Say something like, "If I make a booking, then I'll give you X. If you make the booking, I'll pay you Y (with X and Y referring to different commission amounts)."

In my opinion, Jack Simpson, a real estate agent and property manager, has developed one of the best partnership programs available to owners. For the weeks that he books for owners, he takes full commission. But for the weeks that owners book, he takes no commission. However, he agrees to facilitate the cleaning and maintenance on the owner-booked weeks and charges them the appropriate fees. Through my traveling and speaking, owners have told me that this kind of partnership can be found in other areas. Search for an arrangement like this; it's the best I've heard of.

In a partnership, what is a reasonable amount of commission for each of you? Frequently, owners arrange to get a reduction of 10 to 15 percent of their regular commission rates. For example, if the company's commission is 40 percent, the reduced commission would be 25 to 30 percent. Are company representatives likely to object to that? No, because they realize that the vacationers you bring in are guests they wouldn't have attracted otherwise.

While this arrangement may not be ideal, you'll be surprised at how open companies might be to your suggestions. After all, you both have an interest in making money so you'll likely find a lot of room to negotiate the details. You can negotiate which weeks the company is responsible for various management issues. For example, will it facilitate the cleaning and maintenance on the weeks that you book, also? You can generally hammer out the finer points of the partnership fairly easily.

Control Weeks of Use

When you set up a partnership program, you also can spell out the conditions for rental seasons that are acceptable to you, not to the management company. This addresses the management company's policies that require you to sign a contract stating you will allow them to rent a certain number of weeks and limit when you can use your own property (for example, during Christmas, spring break, and Fourth of July). In your negotiations, be sure to set aside the time *you* want for your vacation or some special event. After all, what good is owning a vacation home if you don't retain control over when you get to enjoy your own property?

Handle Bookings Yourself

I recommend, though, that you consider handling all the bookings yourself. This is the best way to keep your management company honest.

Here's the specific scenario you want to avoid: You advertise and take inquiries for your property. You speak with a renter who says, "I want to book your place." Then you give that person the number of the management company and say, "Call this number and tell the representative that you want to rent the Karpinski unit #1232." The renter calls and just makes one comment about wanting a place with two fireplaces instead of one, but continues to say, "We spoke with Christine and have decided her place will be fine." Now, the representative takes this opportunity to say, "Well, I have another property down the road that has two fireplaces and it's available that same week." Guess what, my friend? You just lost out on that valuable rental!

Collecting Rental Money

When you rent out your place yourself, you're accepting all the payments yourself. And when you set up a partnership program with a management company, I suggest you also accept the payments yourself. That way, you get all *your* money up front. Compare that with the practice of most management companies that usually don't send your money until 30 days after month's end. Some don't even send out the money until it has cleared the credit card companies, which can take up to 90 days.

As one season melts into the next, you will become more creative and proficient at finding the best mix for you. And if you're able to avoid paying some of the commission, you can use that money to take a vacation yourself!

9

ADVERTISING YOUR RENTAL PROPERTY

The advertising industry spends billions every year promoting all sorts of trendy (and sometimes useless) products to prospective buyers—and succeeds with effectiveness. As Jack Simpson, a seasoned real estate columnist, once wrote: "Advertising is a powerful tool . . . without it, your business is dead. If you ever run out of money, cut your pay, cut your staff, quit paying your bills, but *don't* ever stop advertising. Because if you do, it's all over!"

Another wise businessman said: "Eighty percent of all advertising is wasted. The trick is to find out what draws the other 20 percent in."

HOW TO GET RENTERS TO LOOK FOR YOU

Indeed, being successful in the vacation rental business requires that you advertise with effectiveness. Ideally, you want your renters to look for you; you don't want to have to look for your renters. They're looking to find properties and you want them to find yours easily.

Print Advertising

In this information age, newspapers still play a role in advertising for many businesses. But in major metropolitan areas, advertising prices are prohibitively high. And, let's face it, few people these days spend time and effort scouring big-city newspapers looking for vacation rentals. Your print advertising dollar would be better spent creating and distributing an ad sheet in your office, in a church bulletin, or in small community newspaper. These forms of advertising have proven to be effective and inexpensive. In some locales, the local newspaper can be the *only* way to find certain rental properties. For example, my family wanted to visit a town in upstate New York, but I couldn't find a single rental online. So I dug out the local newspaper and started looking through the classified ads. Sure enough, we eventually found a place advertised for rent.

Internet Advertising

Web sites help vacationers see your property, feel it, touch it, and imagine being there enjoying it themselves. In fact, travel is the number one reason people turn to the Internet. Clearly, the Internet is the most effective place to advertise your vacation rental property. In fact, I have never used print advertising since I started out in 1997. And the good news is that advertising your vacation rental on Web sites can be 100 percent effective in renting your vacation property—if you use them to their fullest extent. And you'll find that doing so costs remarkably little.

You don't have to be a computer whiz to use the Internet. You only have to know how to e-mail and surf the World Wide Web. If you're unsure about how to use your computer to create a Web listing for your vacation property, you can attend classes at learning centers in your community. (See Appendix D for a list of learning centers nationwide.)

You're likely spending time on the Internet surfing the Web. Maybe you're asking, "How in the world can I get my message out there? Won't it get lost?" When you search under the term "vacation rental" you get more than 12 million results! But I assure you, yours won't get lost—if you go about it the right way. For example, New York City is a big city, but with a good map or a competent tour guide, you can go exactly where you want.

As your Internet tour guide, let's examine four different kinds of Web sites:

1. Vacation property listing services (portal sites)
2. Specialized Web sites
3. Universal Web sites
4. Personal property Web sites

VACATION PROPERTY LISTING SERVICES—PORTAL SITES

Vacation property listing services are Web sites that advertise vacation property for "rent by owner" (see Appendix B for a list of Web sites). These vacation property "portal" sites are basically gateways to finding what you want on the Internet.

Think of a portal site as the classified section of your newspaper. If you want to buy a new car, for example, you pick up your local paper and turn to the "used car" classified section. In a similar way, you can regard portal sites as the subtopic in the classified section of the Internet that helps you find a very specific product or service. Yes, it could be like looking for a needle in a haystack, but using search engines makes it easy to find exactly what you're looking for.

Portal sites for vacation rentals do all the search engine rankings for you through key words. How does this work? When people search on the Internet for a vacation rental, they'll likely end up at several of the major portal sites designed precisely for that purpose. And there are hundreds, possibly thousands, of such sites online. (For a list of portal sites, see Appendix B.)

Renters seeking accommodations get in touch with vacation property owners through portal sites. Fees to post your property on these sites range from $50 to $150 a year, although some are free, too. Others charge on a three- to six-month basis, and a few charge by the number of hits or clicks (that is, the number of times a visitor clicks on your listing).

Portal sites take responsibility for doing marketing through search engine ranking. They're specifically designed to help vacationers find properties to rent in particular locations.

For your listings on portal sites, include descriptions and photos of your property, note the number of bedrooms and bathrooms, list the amenities available, and entice prospective renters with information about local attractions and events. Some sites allow you to link to your own personal property Web site (noted later in this chapter).

Just as the classified section of the newspaper limits the size of your ad, portal Web sites may have limited space or fields available for you to fully describe your property. Some specialized Web sites won't allow you to link to a portal Web site page. This is one reason I advocate you also build a personal property Web site for your vacation rental properties.

Some people ask why they should put their listing on portal sites when they have a personal property Web site. Through experience, I have come to this conclusion: In some markets, it's extremely difficult to get your own site ranked high on search engines. Take an area like Orlando, Florida, for example; it would be difficult and expensive to get your Web site high on the search engines because you're competing with Disney World, Epcot Center, Universal Studios, and all the other theme parks and hotels. However, if you owned a cabin near Litchfield, Illinois, that you rent, since there's not much competition for vacation property there, your cabin would easily show up on a search for rental property in Litchfield, Illinois.

Portal Web sites have people working full-time to achieve high rankings on the search engines. According to Hunter Melville of CyberRentals.com, his company spends in excess of $200,000 buying key words in order to have CyberRentals.com come up high on the search engine in hundreds of popular vacation rental markets. Individual owners simply don't have the money or knowledge to have their personal property Web sites consistently show up high in the rankings. So I advocate that you take advantage of the co-op buying power that portal Web sites give to achieve maximum exposure for your property.

> *When I started renting by owner many years ago, I had my own personal property Web site and my properties weren't on any listing services. Back then, if I typed "Destin Florida vacation rentals" into a search engine, often my Web site would come up in the top three results. But today, it would take a lot of work, as well as money, to achieve this.*

Now, you may be saying, "I get e-mail requests directly from my personal property Web site." If so, ask yourself this: "Do I also have it linked from http://www.vacationrentals.com and other portal sites?" Most often, renters found your Web site through the links on these portal Web sites. Don't get me wrong. I still advocate having a personal property Web site for your listings because it can convey much more information about your property than the portal sites allow.

Best Web Sites for Advertising

There is no single answer to the question "What is the best Web site to advertise on?" Each property uniquely draws one type of vacationer but doesn't attract another. To start choosing the best ones for you, find portal Web sites that are directly related to your renters' needs. For your convenience, I've listed my top picks for portal sites in Appendix B. I recommend working with at least one of these four top choices, yet also realize that some of the honorable mention sites may be better for your area or situation. I base my top choices on studies, personal experience, and feedback from clients I've worked with. Then I take into account sites with the least number of complaints, the most effective inquiries leading to bookings, their overall exposure in the marketplace, their site managers' responsiveness to owners' and renters' needs, and their dedication to the industry.

I suggest you list your property on multiple Web sites—three to five of them at least—for maximum exposure. Even listing on three sites costs less than $600 a year. Just with renting your place for one week, you've made back enough to cover the expense.

That being said, some owners don't use any of the bigger sites because they get all their bookings by advertising on a specific site. For example, owners in Hot Springs, North Carolina, only have their listings on a site that features hot springs properties and Web sites devoted to hiking the Appalachian Trail. The size of the Web sites isn't important; what's important is that it easily can be found by the renters.

When determining where to list, *think like your customers.* Are they skiers, scuba divers, or devotees of the nightlife? Do they have children's interests in mind? Is your property near a marina, ski slopes, or casinos? Does it have wheelchair accessibility? Do you allow pets? Do you cater to senior citizens? Look for specialty sites for all these types of properties, and then advertise accordingly.

If you pretend you're a renter looking for your property, what do you do? Go to any search engine and type in key words like "Destin vacation rental." Look at the first few sites on the search results and see if there are other properties on this site in the same area as your property. Contrary to popular belief, it's generally better to be listed on sites that have other properties in your area. Renters like to have choices; if yours is the only property listed in your area, chances are that renters will move on to the next Web site that offers more choices. Don't be shy. Send an e-mail to the owners of a few properties and ask, "How well is this particular Web site working for you?" You may think it's odd to ask competitors for advice, but in this field, most owners are not businesspeople in the ordinary sense. Many of them gladly share their experiences.

How many sites you need to list with comes down to supply and demand. If you're listing a property in a popular destination, you might get away with listing with just one to three portal Web sites. However, if your vacation property is in an obscure area, it would be wise to list with five or more Web sites.

SPECIALIZED WEB SITES

Add variety to your Web site advertising by considering specialized ads that bring people to the site. For example, many vacationers going to Colorado check both the Internet and ski magazines, so owners know to advertise in both.

Specialized Web sites cater to the particular needs, desires, or interests of certain groups of people. Some are devoted to listing vacation properties and others are not. Some have a designated area where you can add your property; on others, site visitors might have to dig to find an area that links to your personal property Web site address.

An example of a specialized site devoted to vacation property listings is http://www.lakehousevacations.com. It connects a specific group of renters with a targeted group of property owners (that is, those who have vacation homes on lakes). Most of these sites function like portal sites, allowing owners to list the details of their property for a yearly fee.

Don't restrict your listing to specialized sites designed specifically for renters. A good alternative would be http://www.fly shop.com, which is *Fly Fisherman Magazine*'s Web site. Its main purpose is to sell the magazine. In addition, visitors find lots of information about fly-fishing, including good fishing destinations. The Web site features a section called "Travel Center." Why not go there and request to add a link to your cabin or vacation home located in a fly-fishing area?

A third type of specialized site draws in vacationers looking for accommodations as well as people visiting it for a special purpose. Examples include chamber of commerce Web sites or local area Web sites. A chamber of commerce site, for example, has area information about shopping, restaurants, local festivals and activities, plus accommodations in that area. This kind of Web site draws people to it for many reasons, not just to look for accommodations. Most chamber Web sites also allow its members a link to a personal Web site, most often a free service to members. How do you become a member? Most chambers only require that you collect sales tax, which you most likely already do. Be sure to take advantage of valuable Web sites like these if they're available in your community.

UNIVERSAL SERVICE WEB SITES

Universal service Web sites offer particular services related to vacation travel—ones that you could include on your Web sites. Here are some examples.

Calendar Web sites. Although most portal Web sites provide calendars, most specialized sites don't, so you'll need an availability calendar to link through to your personal property Web site. The sites RentOneOnline.com and Rentors.org offer universal vacation rental availability calendars that you can access through your personal property Web site.

Mapping Web sites. The most well-known mapping Web site is http://www.mapquest.com, which you can link to your Web site for free. Prospective renters like to know your property's location and how to get there, so linking your Web site to Mapquest or http://maps.google.com and typing in the address makes that possible. A word of caution: Don't include the exact address of your property on a Web site. For example, instead of pointing Mapquest to 123 Sand St., point it to a nearby intersection.

Payment Web sites. If you want to accept electronic payments of any kind, then you can get a PayPal account (no charge) and work through it to accept bank transfers and credit cards (for a fee). Go to http://www.paypal.com for details. Two other sites that offer payment solutions are http://www.rentoneonline.com and http://www.rentors.org.

PERSONAL PROPERTY WEB SITE

A personal property Web site is a site that you (or someone you hire) build and maintain for your vacation property business. This site gives detailed information about your property in one place and provides links to specialized sites and universal services sites. Prospective renters who find a listing for your property at a portal Web site like http://www.vrbo.com want to see more photographs and get more information. Be sure you have plenty of quality photographs and detailed descriptions on your site to help persuade them to rent from you.

However, don't depend on your personal property Web site as your main form of advertising. Understand that, like a brochure, it's a selling tool that describes your property, rules, policies, rates, and so on. Design it to impress potential renters with in-depth information regarding property features.

Another reason I'm an advocate of putting up a personal property Web site is to help you keep your prospects in *your* pocket. When they call, they'll often say they found your listing on the Internet. If you ask which Web site, they say they don't re-member. Here's where you can get into trouble. If they saw the listing on http://www.vacationrentals.com and you sent them to http://www.cyberrentals.com to revisit it, you've just introduced them to a lot more inventory to choose from. Certainly while you've got the attention of those customers, don't let them get away. Instead of sending them back to a portal site, send them to your personal property Web site where only your properties are listed. This is also where you can include specific policies and pro-cedures that portal Web sites don't allow.

Think of your portal sites as the online classified section of the newspaper that lists lots of car ads. Then think of your per-sonal property Web site as the automobile showroom. When you take visitors there, they can see the product more completely. It provides answers to routine questions they'd ask on the phone. This additional information helps them make a better-informed decision.

Setting Up Your Personal Property Web Site

When setting up your personal property Web site, you have two main choices:

1. You can use the Web site space you likely get through your Internet Service Provider (ISP) such as AOL, MSN, and Earthlink, to name a few.
2. You can obtain your own domain name and find a service to host your site.

Web site space through your ISP. When you sign up for Internet service, along with your e-mail address and dial-up cable modem or DSL service, you typically get a small amount of Web site space that you can use to host a personal site. (Check with your ISP; you may have free space available as a subscriber.) To view a person's personal Web site hosted by an ISP, Internet users will have to enter an address like home.e-mailAddress.earthlink .com. *Note:* Sometimes you can purchase a domain name and redirect the address to your ISP. If you do so, be sure to cloak, or hide, the address forwarding so that your chosen domain name remains displayed.

Registering your own domain name. Your second choice—and the one I recommend for developing your personal Web site—is to register your own domain name (Internet address) with an associated e-mail address. For example, my domain name is HowToRentByOwner.com with my e-mail being Christine@How ToRentByOwner.com.

You can purchase domain names for a yearlong period with renewals due each additional year. The cost to register a domain can vary significantly; however, most are $35 a year or less. I recommend checking out http://www.godaddy.com where registrations cost $9 a year.

Once you have registered your domain name, do your homework to find a place to host your domain. You'll find that hosting companies vary greatly in price and in degree of service provided. I suggest you look around for a basic service, especially if you only have one property to list and not a whole store full of products.

Domain name versus ISP-provided site. Why go to the trouble and cost of registering a domain when you have space already at your fingertips through your ISP service? It's because a domain name is permanent (so long as you pay the renewal fee annually), even if you change Internet providers. Remember, each time you change providers, you have to notify people that your e-mail address has changed, and you'll have to move or rebuild your Web site, too. Besides, anyone who has bookmarked your site for future reference gets a dead-end address. If that happens, how would potential guests contact you again?

When Terry and Tim were planning their most recent vacation, they contacted me and told me they'd seen my property for the first time three years ago. They'd looked at my calendar on the site and saw the property was booked during the times they wanted. Since they'd never contacted me, I didn't even know they were interested. But they had bookmarked my Web site on their computer. This year, they saw that my place was available and called me. That demonstrates the advantage of keeping your domain name the same over the years.

Building a personal property Web site with your own domain name builds a brand name (a name people remember to identify *your* rental property). For example, HowToRentByOwner.com is much easier to remember and gives an air of professionalism.

Also consider that your own domain name enhances your property value because when you sell it, you can promote it by saying, "Property with a great rental history and a complete Web site included." It's like you're selling an established business rather than just another property.

Building Your Web Site

To build your own Web site, you can hire an individual (college students typically are reasonably priced), or hire a company (which can be expensive), or do it yourself. "What?" you say. "I have no idea how to do it. I have trouble even programming the VCR! How am I ever going to design my own Web site?"

It's easier than you think. If you can navigate your way through a program such as Microsoft Word, then you can build your own Web site. You can even take a class through a learning center (see Appendix D for a list of learning centers) or through continuing education classes offered by most counties and universities.

I suggest that you go with one of the many online programs that allow you to purchase a domain name as well as develop and maintain your Web site. These all-in-one sites are inexpensive (costing between $5 and $10 a month) and tend to be user-friendly. (Go to my Web site at http://www.HowToRentByOwner.com for an up-to-date list of providers.)

To select a name for your Web site, tie it to the name of your vacation property so it's easy to remember—for example, Hunting Cabin.com or Flyfishing.com—then set up an e-mail address that attaches to the Web site, such as hunt@huntingcabin.com or Dan @flyfishing.com.

WRITING ADVERTISEMENTS FOR PORTALS AND PERSONAL SITES

You'll get lots of ideas for how to write the copy you need to advertise your Web site by following the suggestions in this section.

Location. Don't forget to put specific location information on your advertisements. A descriptive phrase such as "Florida Gulf Coast" is too vague. On the flip side, don't just state the name of the town and write it this way: Location: Destin, Florida. Why? Because many haven't heard of this town and don't have any idea where it is, it's better to write something like "located in Destin, along the Florida Gulf Coast. Destin is between Panama City and Pensacola, along the panhandle of Florida." Be sure the two cities you mention are known cities easily found on a map. If your place is a distance from major cities, still list them and also name local towns. For example, "located in Destin, along the Florida Gulf Coast. Destin is between Panama City and Pensacola on the panhandle of Florida, just three miles from Okaloosa Island and eight miles from Seaside." Be sure to also include the closest airport.

One-line descriptions. When vacationers go to a portal Web site, they find a list of properties to rent in the country, region, and town they want to visit. When they see a screen full of listings (and more), what makes them click on a specific property? If you don't capture their interest, you know they'll continue scanning and scrolling. That's why your one-line description of the property needs to be sharp, strong, and inviting. Look at these two one-liners:

1. View, Private, Close-in, 2 Bd 2 Ba, 3 Fireplaces
2. 2 bedroom mountain cabin

Which one tells more information, which is the one most people would click on? Learn to write your one-line descriptions with the detail and appeal of the first one.

Detailed description. Next, write a second, more detailed description in three to six concise paragraphs. Write enough to interest people but not too much or you'll lose their attention. Here's the description I use for my cabin in Gatlinburg, written by ad writer Amy Greener (see Appendix E for contact information).

Wow . . . Here's everything you could want in a cabin. And if that's not enough, we have another cabin right next door in case you have a group or family gathering. (Between the two cabins, there is sleeping accommodations for 12.) What's more, because we privately own and manage our cabins, you'll be pleasantly surprised by all the extras and special touches.

Located only one and a half miles from Dollywood and Splash Mountain, and easily accessible from the Knoxville, Tennessee, airport (30 miles), our cabins are three miles from the main parkway. You'll love the private location with convenience to Pigeon Forge and Gatlinburg. Nestled in over an acre of land, the cabin has a nice mountain view from the deck.

What sets this cabin apart is not one, but two master suites, each with a fireplace, TV, and corner Jacuzzi. Very few two-bedroom cabins offer two master suites, so couples will appreciate that no one has to compromise! For extra sleeping accommodations, we have a queen-size sofa bed in the main living area. (Kids will love the sofa bed because they can stay up late playing provided video games and watching their favorite shows on DirecTV.) And for the wee little ones, we even have a pack-n-play crib!

The warm, rustic, wood interior and beautiful decor provide the complete cabin experience, while fun extras add to your enjoyment. Play a game of pool, darts, or Scrabble; relax by the natural stone gas fireplace; enjoy a DVD or VHS movie on a rainy night, or discover the ultimate treat of soaking in the covered hot tub after a long, activity-filled day. Even the rocking chairs on the deck beckon you to sit for a moment and enjoy the view.

We also provide a fully equipped kitchen and a barbecue grill. Whether you just want to make a quick breakfast before spending the day at Dollywood or stay in and grill up a feast, you will find the kitchen ready for any task. Plus our washer and dryer mean you can pack lighter—saving more room for shopping "finds" at the outlet stores!

Finally, we welcome good pets (dogs only, please) with prior approval. The cabin's one-acre property is perfect for four-legged guests.

With all the luxuries and extras, you won't want to leave this wonderful cabin. So go ahead . . . spoil yourself! Don't let this one get away! Call or e-mail us if you would like more information. Ask for the owners, Christine and Tom (please see phone numbers below).

Photos. Use eye-catching photographs because, as the old cliché goes, a picture is worth a thousand words. Photos are your number one selling point. Learn to take great photos yourself (a full chapter, "Picture Perfect Rental Photos," in the author's book *How to Rent Vacation Properties by Owner* explains staging, lighting, focal points, and more on how to take photos that "sell" a property). Or you can hire a professional photographer for the interior and exterior scenes. *Note:* Remember, photos have copyrights. If you're using a photo you didn't take yourself, be sure to get written permission from the photographer and/or publication in which you found the photo.

Contact phone numbers. It is an absolute must that you include your phone number, both on the portal Web site and on your own personal Web site. I know you might feel a bit squeamish about your privacy and be uncomfortable with the idea of posting your phone number out there for the whole world to see. But keep in mind that this is a business. Would you want to do business with a company that had no phone number? Probably not. So you have to provide a number where the renters can easily reach you.

In addition to the phone numbers, be sure to include your time zone (for example, Eastern Standard Time or EST). Also state the hours you'd be willing to take phone calls. Consider listing your cell phone number, too. But I don't recommend purchasing a toll-free number for reservations. Otherwise, it looks too much like a business number and renters may not hesitate to call you at 3 AM!

E-mail address. Be sure to include a way for vacationers to contact you through e-mail on your personal property site. Some owners choose not to show their e-mail addresses but ask for the prospective renter's address through a "contact me" button. Many portal Web sites hide the owner's e-mail address and require the renters to inquire through their own Web sites. This is for your protection and helps reduce spamming.

Rates. Quote all rates, including nightly, weekly, and seasonal discounted rates. This information should go both on the portal sites and on your own personal Web site. Don't leave any rates ambiguous. People coming from different markets may not be familiar with the prices. For example, someone who's accustomed to renting a cabin in Tennessee for $1,000 a week and decides to rent a cabin at Lake Tahoe might be surprised to find out how much more expensive a comparable Tahoe property costs.

Use a list format to communicate rates because lists are easy to read. Also use dashes to set off each item and asterisks for special notations. Ellipses are great to draw the eye across the page and prevent a cluttered look. Make sure your writing is clear and detailed to make it easy to understand your rates. (For pricing details, go to Chapter 7.)

Additional charges and restrictions. You should also quote any fees, taxes, or additional charges. It's always a good policy to be as up front and honest as possible. Some portal Web sites will have a field for these, others will not, so you will have to input the information manually. In either case, make sure that you include this information not only on your personal Web site, but also on the portal site. Additional charges could include pets, deposits, cleaning fees, or a variety of other things.

Restrictions would be things that you do not allow—the "don't even call me if . . ." items. The most common restrictions are no rentals to anyone under age 25, no pets, no smoking, and minimum-length stays.

Amenities. Many portal Web sites have check boxes for things that you have in your property, and some require you to just write them in. Don't overlook anything here; many renters want to know about the conveniences of home and more. This is where you spell out everything you have. These would be things like a pool, tennis courts, hot tub, full kitchen, etc. There also may be specifics such as linens provided, coffeemaker, toaster, etc.

Being a longtime owner, I am always amazed by what "things" are important to renters. I've had questions all over the board, from "Do you have a washer and dryer?" to "Do you have martini glasses?" If you have it, list it.

Local attractions. Don't forget the local attractions. People want to know what there is to do in your area. For example, many people might consider the Myrtle Beach, South Carolina, area as strictly beach. Renters might not realize there are several attractions that would appeal as much as the beach, such as a nearby battleship, an impressive aquarium, a golfer's haven, and many other not-so-well-known local attractions.

Calendar. It's important to display an availability calendar and keep it up-to-date. Some renters only look at properties with this feature. It will save both you and your renters a lot of time. Here's an astounding and true statistic: The calendar feature on one of my Web sites truly changed my rental life! I went from 1,400 "Sorry, I'm booked" responses in a year to only 200! *A word of caution: Do not mark your calendars "booked" until after you receive the deposit.*

Testimonials. Be sure to add comments that you've received from past renters on your site. If you just started and have none yet, omit testimonials for now and add this feature later. It takes a little patience and having a reputation as a good property first; then the compliments will follow.

10

BUYING AND HOLDING YOUR VACATION HOME

In a strong economy, vacation home properties have a higher appreciation rate than primary homes, with supply and demand being the most prevalent factor. Because only so much beachfront, lakefront, ski slope, and mountain homes with views are available, their numbers are fewer than the buyers who want to purchase them. Therefore, they tend to be priced higher than homes in city neighborhoods. And that trend appears to be continuing. Studies show that while home values appreciated 9 to 12 percent a year on average, vacation homes went up 22 percent. As real estate journalist Broderick Perkins wrote in a *Realty Times* column, "Existing and emerging supply-and-demand economics likely will continue to drive the lucrative vacation home market and along with it, the returns on vacation home investments."

LETTING YOUR VACATION HOME APPRECIATE

How can people afford vacation homes when they're so expensive? Many do so by purchasing what they can afford now and "buying up" later, using the appreciation gained in their initial purchases to afford the next price level. Don't get overwhelmed by this thought. You probably started with a small "starter" home, and at some transition point in your life, you moved up to a bigger house. During the time you owned your first home, prices appreciated and your equity built up. Then you sold it and used both the equity and appreciation to be able to buy up. When people buy up, usually the cost of the house changes significantly, but the payment doesn't.

Rob and Becky bought their first home for $80,000. They owned it for seven years and sold it for $100,000. Their new home cost $160,000, which was double their initial purchase. But their mortgage payment stayed the same because the proceeds from the sale of their starter home paid for a substantial amount toward the purchase price of their new home.

This same principle applies to your vacation home: Wait until your first property appreciates and accumulates equity. Then you'll have the leverage and the buying power to purchase another home—to buy up. As noted in Chapter 4 on financing options, you can use your current investments to make more money by putting the money into assets—vacation properties—that have a history of appreciating in value.

Part of Your Investment Portfolio

Compare the average annual appreciation of 22 percent on a vacation home to buying a mutual fund that typically yields 7 to

10 percent annually if you leave it in the stock market over a length of time.

I certainly accept that diversifying investments is a good way to go. I think these appreciation percentages convey that the right vacation properties should be considered a strong part of your diversified investment portfolio. Your property may not cover current expenses in the short run, but you'll still realize appreciation in the long run.

Ashley purchased an existing furnished beachfront condo for $165,000 in 1999, putting down $8,250. She had positive cash flow from day one, earning $23,000 (above and beyond all the expenses) over the first five-year period. She earned $2,000 the first year, $3,500 the second year, $4,100 the third year, $6,000 the fourth year, and $7,400 the last year. She sold the condo in 2003 for $300,000. So over the entire time of ownership, tracking the initial costs and expenses, Ashley realized a total of $149,750 from the sale. Instead of having just the amount of her initial down payment of $8,250, she has $149,750 to put toward her next purchase and can therefore afford a much bigger place.

Cynthia's Condo to Flip

Cynthia bought a two-bedroom, two-bath preconstruction beachfront condo in Florida during the presale stage. The purchase price was $195,000. At the time of signing the hard contract, she needed a down payment of 20 percent of the purchase price, so she put down $19,500 (10 percent) and had a secured letter of credit for the additional 10 percent of the required 20 percent deposit. Three years later, Cynthia closed on the property the day it was finished and sold it two hours later for $325,000. Her initial cash investment of $19,500 became $130,000, earning her $110,500 in three years. That calculates to be an annualized return of 88.20 percent, with a return for the three-year period of 566.59 percent.

Harry's Condo to Rent Out

Harry purchased a similar two-bedroom, two-bath condo in the same complex as Cynthia and at the same price and time. He spent $16,000 to furnish his unit and set out to rent it. In the first year, rentals were sparse, and he had to pay $5,000 in out-of-pocket expenses to cover the mortgage and other costs. The second year, rentals picked up and he almost reached break-even cash flow, paying $1,000 in out-of-pocket expenses. After two years of renting, he sold his unit for $400,000. Coupled with the two years of rental loss and the cost to furnish the property, it cost him around $22,000 in extra cash investment.

Let's examine what happened. Harry invested a total of $41,500 (down payment, furnishings, and negative cash flow for the first two years) over five years and it became $164,500, which is an annualized return of 52.61 percent. His return for the five-year period was 727.78 percent.

While these numbers are certainly high and represent best-case scenarios, these kinds of investments really do exist in the marketplace. You just have to do extensive research to find them.

Generally speaking, your vacation property in high-traffic resort areas will pay for itself because potential renters keep coming. Surprisingly, even after the tragic events of September 11, 2001, the vacation rental market remained strong. In the panic period that followed 9/11, people declared they wanted more fulfillment out of living, realizing that their lives could end as suddenly as those who died that day. People in general have tended to put vacations high on their priority lists. If they have to travel on the cheap or go into debt, they still take vacations.

Safety Net

As Steven learned with his first vacation home investment, a smart, conservative approach can provide a financial safety net over time.

Steven bought his first property and it appreciated at a steady rate over five years. He took out a home equity line of credit on this property to pay for a down payment on a second property, basically leveraging the amount of the appreciation instead of the full value of the property. Being a highly conservative investor, he had a goal to never exceed 80 percent loan to value. His theory was that if the real estate market "tanked," he'd have a 20 percent cushion at all times. That meant the real estate market could drop 20 percent and he could still get out of his investments easily without taking a loss.

Specifically, Steve paid $100,000 for his first property, putting down $20,000 and carrying an $80,000 mortgage. Five years later, the home had appreciated to $150,000, giving him $70,000 in equity ($20,000 initial down payment plus $50,000 in appreciation). He took out a $40,000 home equity loan, leaving a total mortgaged amount of $120,000. This way, he had 20 percent equity in this property, so even though it had appreciated to $150,000, he only had $120,000 in debt. If he had mortgaged 100 percent of it, he could face a loss when he sold it if the market dropped significantly. (To round the numbers for this example, amortized mortgage payments are not factored in.)

The way Steven looked at it, the market could drop by 20 percent, and he still wouldn't lose his shirt. Using his first property as a safety net, Steven has continued this method of conservative leveraging to purchase more and more properties without taking huge risks.

Vacation Homes for Retirement

Because of the appreciation factor, you might assume your primary residence will be a good investment in the long run, but is it really true? After all, while most investments are designed to be bought and sold, you wouldn't sell your primary home like you would stocks and bonds, because you still would need a place to live. So I never view my primary home as an investment. However, when you buy a second home, it often is viewed as an investment in tandem, living in one and renting out the other. Or, as an alternative, you can always live in one and sell the other, living off the proceeds of the sale. Among people who retired in the U.K., those who had second homes were much better off after their pension funds decreased than those who only owned one home.

Jack and Maryanne bought their suburban home when they were newly married. They'd always believed they would sell their first house and move somewhere else when they retired. Over the years, though, they'd settled into their neighborhood and brought up their children in this home. Naturally, they developed an emotional attachment to it. Because they regarded their home as an investment, they sank all their money into it and paid off the mortgage.

Even though they thought they would buy a smaller retirement-community home in their golden years, when the time came, they didn't really want to leave. The home they once viewed as an investment couldn't be considered as such because they weren't willing to let it go. If they had purchased a second home earlier in their lives and never moved to that second home, they could have sold it and enjoyed the proceeds.

1031 EXCHANGES TO DEFER CAPITAL GAINS TAX

Before 1979, it was complicated to buy and sell properties in a way that deferred paying capital gains tax. That year, the Starker decision in the U.S. 9th Circuit Court of Appeals changed the rules and made it possible for investors to have more time to find a desirable property after selling one. The transaction, properly executed, would qualify for tax-deferred status. Treasury regulations passed in 1991 validated and simplified this process. As a result, the Internal Revenue Code Section 1031 (commonly referred to as a 1031 exchange among property owners) states this: "No gain or loss shall be recognized if property held for productive use in a trade or business or for investment purposes is exchanged solely for property of a like kind." For real estate investors in particular, the 1031 exchange code allows them latitude in their choice of investments. They can exchange raw land for a rental home, an apartment complex for vacation properties, rental houses for an office building, and similar investments. The rules for 1031 exchanges require that a replacement property be identified within 45 days of the sale of the first property to realize the tax-deferred benefits.

Your real estate agent and/or tax advisor will give you full details on how 1031 exchanges can work to your benefit as a vacation home investor. With the funds you thought you'd have to pay in taxes, you can invest in your next property!

In a previous example, Ashley had sold her property and realized a net profit of $149,750. She had a choice. She could pocket that money, but then she'd have to pay capital gains tax. Or she could use it to buy another property using a 1031 exchange. Doing so would be wise because she could defer paying taxes on her profits to a time when her overall taxable income will likely be lower (i.e., in retirement).

LONG-TERM VERSUS SHORT-TERM RENTALS

How do you determine if you should stick with vacation rentals or commit to a long-term lease for your vacation home? On the other side of the coin, should you consider turning your long-term leased property into a vacation rental?

The answers lie in your projected income numbers plus your personal preferences.

Key Questions to Ask

A lot of personal factors come into consideration when you compare the benefits of long-term versus short-term rentals. Here are key questions to consider as you determine if managing short-term vacation home rentals fits your lifestyle:

- How much annual income could you realize with long-term rentals compared with short-term ones?
- Do you wish to use the place for your own vacation? If so, you'll need to block out certain weeks for yourself, knowing you won't receive income during those weeks.
- Do you have the cash to lay out for furnishings? Does the income potential outweigh the initial costs of buying the furnishings?
- How much will it cost for utilities, maintenance, and other expenses that you wouldn't incur with long-term rentals?
- How many off-season rentals do you project you'll have?
- What's the relative effect of wear and tear on the property?
- Do you have the time and desire to educate yourself in all the aspects of short-term rentals?
- Do you have the time to devote to managing short-term rentals? (Clearly, it takes more time and effort on your part than long-term leasing would.)

Here's an example of a hybrid solution mixing short-term and long-term leasing.

> I own a condo in Destin, Florida, where snowbirds typically pay $1,500 a month to stay for the months of January, February, and March. January and February tend to be quiet vacation rental months, but during March, I can rent out my place for $1,500 a week at least three of the four weeks. Is it worthwhile to let renters stay the full three months when you can yield the same money for three weeks?
>
> Straddling both options, here's what I do. I let the snowbirds stay from January 1 to March 15, which left me with two peak-renting weeks in the month. I regarded this as the best of both worlds. I have renters in the otherwise "empty" season. And I make at least an equal amount of money, but more often I make even more.

Don't get me wrong; in many cases, it's better financially to bank on short-term rentals, but just make sure you understand the differences (pro and con) between leasing your home for weekly vacations and long-term rentals. Review the objectives you set out for yourself when you first bought your vacation home. Determine what has changed and how you might have to make different decisions going forward.

Part Four

ENJOYING YOUR VACATION PROPERTY

11

MAINTAINING YOUR PROPERTY (FROM AFAR)

Ask vacation property owners why they hesitate to "rent by owner" and the answer is almost always the same: They fear the unknown. How do I deal with cleaning and maintenance issues long distance? What happens when the toilet clogs or the heater breaks?

Think about it this way. How often do things go wrong in your primary home? Okay, I know it's frustrating to answer a question with a question, but when things go wrong, how do you get them fixed? You simply call a repairman. Isn't it just as easy for you to pick up the phone and make a call as it would be for an on-site management company? And to minimize having to make those repair calls, you can do a lot to prevent potential problems. Read on! You'll find tips throughout this chapter to help you do just that.

CLEANING CHALLENGES

Your cleaning staff is your lifeline to prosperity in this business. Your cleaners help you fill in the distance gap because they're the eyes and ears to your property. Without them, none of your renters would ever want to stay in your place.

Do you have nightmares that a renter will show up and find your place dirty? Sure, you could set it up so that your renters clean the property themselves rather than hire a cleaning staff, but you give up control when you do this. Is that something you really want to do? After all, your renter's idea of "clean" probably isn't the same as yours.

I've found that the "clean it yourself" system only works in cottage and cabin settings when renters are required to bring their own bedding and linens. Even then, owners are generally not satisfied with the level of cleanliness afterward.

But if your place is 100 miles away, you certainly can't go and clean it every time a renter leaves! Face facts: You have to hire some *person* or some *company* to take care of cleaning your property. It's *your* reputation on the line. The idea is to build rapport with each and every vacationer, and if they're satisfied with their experience, they'll likely return. And if you're lucky, they'll tell their friends, too.

Hard to Find?

Okay. You've heard that good help is hard to find. To find housekeepers, first look right outside your front door. Literally! Visit your property on a weekend and go outside at the time when most renters check out. I can almost guarantee that your neighbors have hired cleaning services. All you have to do is talk to the people cleaning their properties and ask them if they would consider working for you. Even if your neighbors use a management company, these workers are usually willing to pick up jobs on the side.

What if the cleaning people you talk with would love to work for you but don't have time? Then consider staggering your check-out time so they can clean both your place and your neighbor's. Remember, you make the rules; you don't have to set checkout at 10 AM and check-in at 3 PM. Make the change to suit your cleaning people's schedules. If they are subcontractors of a management company (not actual employees), chances are good they'll be happy to have another job that's convenient for them. It's definitely worth looking into.

When I purchased my new cabins in Tennessee, I found a housekeeper through the Internet. I went to http://www.vrbo .com and found other owners who rent cabins in my area. I called an owner and asked for a referral. (Don't overlook your fellow owners when looking for resources.) Getting to know your neighbors is always a bonus because you can trade favors. As one owner strongly advised, "Once you find great maintenance people, do nice things for them to keep them."

Another good, yet often overlooked source for finding cleaning people is the local church. Frequently, a pastor or minister knows someone who can use some extra work. Make a few phone calls, introduce yourself, and be resourceful. Certainly don't buy into the cliché, "It's impossible to find good help these days."

Many people have found good cleaning referrals through their real estate agents. Some owners have had success going to local hardware stores and reading handwritten ads on the bulletin boards.

The way I have found all my housekeepers is from referrals. I go to vacation rental portal sites and look for other property owners in my area. I pick up the phone and call them. I ask them about their housekeepers and get a referral. Then, once I contact these housekeepers, I check their references.

Individual or Company?

Should you hire an individual or a company? I wish I had an easy answer to this question, but there are benefits and potential problems that come with both options.

On the upside, you can find cleaning services easily because they're listed in the phone book and other directories. In most cases, hiring a cleaning service costs less than contracting with individuals, and they tend to make sure people show up consistently. Because services have multiple crews of employees, they can make sure someone is always available to cover for any absent workers.

But the downside is that often different people are cleaning your place each week so they don't become familiar with it. Also, large cleaning services work in volume, and their workers rarely take as much time caring for your individual needs as independent cleaners do. Generally, they have a set list of duties they perform and won't deviate from that list.

Individual cleaners, on the other hand, usually take more time to do the work and pay more attention to details and specific requests. Most will even do light maintenance such as changing lightbulbs and furnace filters. They also tend to be better at telling you about possible concerns in your property like a dripping faucet or a damaged wall. When seeking housekeepers, good communication skills is the number one criterion I insist on. Their ability to do an excellent job becomes secondary.

I have hired both companies and individuals to clean my properties. Overall, I've had better luck with individual cleaners, but it might take a few tries to find the right workers. Regardless of which option you choose, be sure to compile names and contact information in your Rolodex as a backup if your cleaners simply don't show up. Again, a housekeeper's ability to communicate with me is number one. Recently, I was faced with a dilemma. I had a housekeeper who cleans better than anyone I have ever known, but she didn't respond to e-mails that I'd sent informing her of dates for cleaning. After receiving a complaint from our renter about low water pressure, I contacted her continually for a week before I reached her. I found out the pump on the well failed at a time when I was expecting guests to arrive the next day. Unfortunately, I lost a whole week of valuable time to get the well up and running because of her lack of response. Coupled with other times where communication was lacking, it pained me to fire her over communication issues. I ended up switching to a cleaning company that had excellent response time and gave me just as acceptable cleaning.

EXPECTATIONS FOR CLEANING STAFF

Create and post a list of expectations for your cleaning staff somewhere inside your property. The back of a closet door works well. Don't worry about hiding your instructions from view of your renters. I think it's okay for them to see that you have high expectations for the people who clean your place. Here's a sample list to start with. Customize it for your property.

Kitchen

Clean cabinets, table, and chairs. Clean, scrub, and sanitize sinks, countertops, and backsplashes. Clean range top and wipe inside of oven. Clean inside and outside of refrigerator and microwave oven. Clean inside of toaster and coffeemaker. Wash floor. Empty dishwasher and quickly organize cupboards. Restock auto dish detergent, liquid dish soap, coffee filters, and trash bags. Put out two clean dishtowels and new dishrag/sponge.

Living Room

Dust windowsills and ledges. Dust furniture, blinds, picture frames, knickknacks, ceiling fan, and lamps. Vacuum carpets or wash floor. Vac-

uum furniture including under seat cushions. Check sofa bed for dirty linens. Wash windows on glass doors. Empty and clean wastebaskets. Leave clean linens for the sofa bed.

B *a t h r o o m s*

Clean, scrub, and sanitize showers and bathtubs, vanity, sinks, and backsplashes. Clean mirrors. Clean and sanitize toilets. Polish chrome. Wash floors and tile walls. Empty wastebasket. Replenish hand soap. Supply clean linens: three hand towels, three washcloths, three bath towels, and one shower mat.

O *ther* **A** *reas*

Check that washer and dryer are empty; clean lint trap on dryer. Check lightbulbs; change them if necessary. Once a month, change furnace filter. Wipe patio set, clean barbeque grill. Notify owner immediately if you notice any damages or missing items, or if the property was left excessively dirty.

PROPER MAINTENANCE

Maintenance done properly will make your rentals run smoothly, but if it's done poorly, it will make your life difficult. Don't make the mistake of thinking you'll call in maintenance people only when something is broken. With your vacation property, I advocate doing preventative maintenance on *everything* you possibly can. I know you've heard this phrase countless times before, but it bears repeating here: An ounce of prevention is worth a pound of cure.

Here's my rule of thumb: Anticipate all your problems up front and fix them before they become an issue. With this mindset, you'll definitely view vacation property ownership as a business venture. That means don't get worked up about spending

$75 twice a year to have your furnace cleaned. What's $75 compared to costs for having it break down and losing valuable rentals? I promise, taking care of standard maintenance issues regularly will make your life easier.

Preventative maintenance can make things work more efficiently and last longer. I have always been diligent about calling my heating and air repairman, Jeff, twice a year. I'm not sure what he does besides charge me $60. Does he blow out the line and check the Freon? It doesn't really matter. About two and a half years ago, I noticed all of my neighbors replacing their condensers (they're pretty hard to miss in a condo in Florida all lined up like little soldiers outside the building). Mine lasted longer because I kept up with my preventative maintenance. And when it came time to replace it (from afar), I was much more comfortable when Jeff called and said, "Christine, I have bad news. It costs $1,400 for a new condenser, and you need one." Had I not worked with Jeff for seven years, you bet I would have been calling around for a second opinion.

I advocate hiring a maintenance person to oversee your property on a continuing basis. This works particularly well for people who live far from their second home and can't visit more than once or twice a year. I think you'll discover that maintenance people are much easier to source than good cleaning people. Use the same tactics for finding them as you did to source your cleaners, choosing either companies or individuals to hire locally.

Exactly how much should you have your regular maintenance person do? As much as you feel you need. Some people have a maintenance person come to their property each time a guest leaves to check on things such as lightbulbs, furnace filters, leaky faucets, and so on. Others scout any problems and notify them and/or their maintenance person if need be. Experiment and find out what works best for your situation.

Pooling Your Resources

Don't overlook the fact that your neighbors are also renting. You may be able to pool your resources and find someone who you can all hire together. Condominium complexes usually have on-staff maintenance people. Check with them and see if they'd like to moonlight. One condominium complex where I own a vacation home has so many self-managing owners that the association found a full-time person to work for them only.

Here's what one resourceful owner did.

Ed and his wife live in New York. They own a vacation property on Grand Cayman Island. Ed decided to rent by owner because a lot of his neighbors were doing it successfully. He was apprehensive about doing it, though, because of the maintenance aspect of managing rentals. How was he supposed to fix anything from New York?

Ed came up with an ingenious solution to this problem. In Grand Cayman, most properties are booked 40-plus weeks a year, so rental revenue is high, but so are management commissions. Because six other people in his complex were renting by owner, Ed decided that they could band together and hire one person to oversee all their properties. If they could hire one person full-time, then each owner would be responsible to pay two months of this person's salary. When other owners in their complex learned what these six owners were doing, they got interested in the idea, too. In the end, 12 owners agreed to each pay one month of this maintenance person's salary. With that money, they had the satisfaction of not worrying about maintaining their properties.

DEALING WITH MISHAPS AND DAMAGES

For the most part, I don't get calls for small mishaps that affect my properties. I find that renters are willing to do quick-solve maintenance themselves, and I rarely even hear about them.

Don't get me wrong. I'm *not* advocating that you have your renters do your maintenance for you; you still have to do preventative maintenance up front. But I've never had to deal with a stopped-up toilet. I keep a plunger handy and the renters just use it. They know I live 400 miles away so they don't call me for minor issues like that. Certainly, fixing problems like a broken washing machine or a broken well (and both have happened to me) can present hurdles. But in these cases, I simply call a repairman, just like I would at home. I keep a copy of the area's phone book nearby so I can source someone quickly. The renters or my cleaning staff let the repairmen into my property and the work gets done without much fanfare.

Yes, this might be an inconvenience for renters, but they usually understand. The bottom line is that these problems don't happen often. And when they do, I compensate the renters for their inconvenience by either refunding all or a portion of the rent or taking a percentage off their next stay. And for some funny reason, most of the renters who encountered problems while they were renting my place are my most loyal repeat renters. I cannot figure out why.

More often than not, things go wrong because the renters themselves have damaged something, usually by mistake. Most renters act responsibly about any damages they have caused. And given the proper tools, most prefer to just fix or solve the problem themselves. This story shows how two owners handled a tricky maintenance issue.

Mike and Michelle own a cabin in the Pennsylvania mountains, and they live in New Jersey. They rented their cabin to a family with children. One night, the renters called to say that their son had been leaning back in his chair (you've seen this before, no doubt) and fell backward. The boy wasn't hurt, but the chair put a small hole in the wall as it fell. The father had noticed some drywall spackle under the sink, so he called the owner and asked if it was all right for him to just fix the hole himself. He also asked if there was some touch-up paint somewhere. What a dream renter!

What do you suppose went through this renter's mind before he called Mike and Michelle? The first thing he probably thought was, "How much is this mishap going to cost us?" Renters are especially resistant to paying a damage fee if they can easily fix the problem themselves. Frankly, they don't want to get socked with damage charges any more than you want the damages. I like to make it easy for them to deal with mishaps on their own.

Major Damage or Theft

I bet you're thinking, "I live far away, how would I even know if there were any serious damages to my vacation home?" Trust me, it rarely happens.

But this is why you need to have good communication with your cleaning staff. Instruct the cleaners to call you immediately after something happens. Keep a Polaroid or a disposable camera in your owner's locked closet along with a self-addressed stamped envelope (some housekeepers carry digital cameras and will e-mail you the photos immediately). If there is damage, have your cleaner take photos and send them to you so you have proof of the damage and a way to assess the cost. It should go without saying that you will not refund the damage deposit until you know how much you are owed. Make a note not to rent to those people again.

One time, my renters broke my bed frame. (Don't ask–I don't want to think about how.) Now, of course, having a bed is a necessity for the next renter, so I asked my cleaning service to send one of her employees to the local mattress store and purchase a new frame. I offered to pay that person's hourly salary for taking care of this, which I did. And I took the money for the frame and that time out of the deposit from those *renters. When I sent the unused portion of the deposit, I mailed a letter stating I was keeping $71.54 of their deposit for the broken bed. I attached receipts for remedied damages and also sent a copy of the rental rules that they signed when they booked. I took a moment to highlight the section on the rules that referred to damage deposits. This cleared up the matter.*

Minor Damage or Theft

Should you worry about every little thing like a broken glass or lost silverware? No. You can't micromanage your place. In the grand scheme of things, these are minor expenses you have to absorb as part of owning a rental property.

I suggest you tell your renters that if they break anything, it's their responsibility to replace it. This is much easier than collecting money. This way, the items will be in place for the next renter. I have a policy for broken items: Replace them with items of equal quality.

I always make it a practice to say to my guests: "This is my second home. I live 400 miles away. I can't worry about every little broken item. If you break something that you feel the next renter would need, like the coffeepot, I would prefer you buy a new one. This way I don't have to try to figure out how much to charge you (out of your deposit) and my next renters have what they need. If you break one plate, don't worry about it, but if you break the whole stack, be sure to replace them." I've found that most renters are quite comfortable with this policy.

Cleanliness Problems

Your renters have checked out. Shortly after, you get a phone call from your cleaning service saying your renters left the place a total mess. Beer cans everywhere, crayon on the walls, a huge stain on the carpet. Use your imagination; it can get bad.

But instead of getting upset, remember your objective: preparing the place quickly for the people checking in later that day. Do whatever it takes. If it means calling a carpet cleaner to come out immediately, then do so. If it means six hours of cleaning time rather than two, then so be it. If your next renters show up before the cleaning has been completed, instruct your housekeepers to tell them to go out to lunch or dinner at your expense. As for covering the costs (I think you guessed this one), take all costs out of the security deposit, including the dinner you had to buy for the next renters. It's a cost associated with the damages made. But never consider this as an opportunity for you to make more money; you only want to cover your costs.

> My housekeeper showed up at my vacation property and called me immediately to say someone had smoked cigars inside. The No Smoking policy is clearly stated on my Web sites, in my rental rules, on the sign on my front door, and on the framed note that says, "Our home is non-smoking. Please respect it. Feel free to use the ashtray located under the kitchen sink to smoke outside on the patio."
>
> But apparently, these renters ignored all. How would I get rid of the smell? It was nearly impossible to air out the place in the five hours between checkout and check-in. So I took all the steps necessary to get everything cleaned and paid for dinner for the next guests, too.
>
> When I sent the letter with the deposit refund and copy of the extra cleaning receipts, the people called and unequivocally denied that they smoked in the property. They admitted they smoked, but claimed they did so outside. They protested having to pay the charges.
>
> This suddenly became a "he said, she said" situation. Should I believe what the renters said or what my housekeeper said? Maybe they did smoke outside but left the sliding door open and the smoke blew in. Or maybe they smoked outside all week long, and as they packed up, Dad had a stogie in his mouth while coming in and out.

What did I do? I stood behind my housekeeper. I explained to the renter that I was sorry, but my loyalties have to be with her. She had worked for me for years and had never made a call like this before. Because I'm not able to physically be there, she is responsible for making judgment calls.

The renter asked if she could then have my housekeeper's phone number so she could discuss this with her. I said no but offered to have her sign a letter stating the damages. In the end, the renter wasn't pleased, but I stood firm. Although I still don't know the real story, I have no reason to disbelieve what my housekeeper said.

PREVENTATIVE STEPS

Below is a list of preventative maintenance procedures you can follow, as well as items you should have on hand for any accidental damages. Follow this list and make sure everything is in working order (especially items that you advertised in your promotions). Be sure to keep good records of all maintenance activities and expenses. I suggest using an organizing system like my *Vacation Rental Organizer* (http://www.HowToRentByOwner .com), a 144-page organizer that helps you track your bookings, manage guest information and phone numbers, log expenses and organize receipts, track inventory, and maintain contact information for service providers.

Here are the essentials:

- Have a copy of the local phone book for your vacation property destination in your permanent home so you can call appropriate maintenance contractors.
- Write down the make, model, and serial numbers of all major appliances. Then, if you need to schedule a service call, you have the information the repair company needs on hand.

- Consider purchasing extended warranties on major appliances, especially washers and dryers. These appliances tend to get used above and beyond normal.
- Have your dryer vent cleaned regularly. (Or when you visit, take your leaf blower and blow it out yourself.)
- Clean the condenser coils on your refrigerator.
- Have your furnace/air conditioner cleaned and checked two times a year.
- Change furnace filters at least once a month.
- Schedule regular chimney and fireplace cleaning and inspections. General rule of thumb: Do it after a cord of wood gets burned. Or for gas logs, once a year.
- Clean out the screens on your faucets and showerheads, especially in areas that have wells and hard water.
- Consider replacing high-water-consumption appliances with water-saving appliances (e.g., toilets, front-load washing machines, dishwashers, and shower heads).
- Clean out sink and tub drains regularly. To do this, unscrew the stopper in sinks and bathtubs and clean out the debris. Loose hair is the most common cause of slow and clogged drains.
- Consider installing a kitchen sink disposal.
- Inspect breaker panels and plug receptacles at least once every two years, especially in salt-water areas. Salt corrodes wiring and causes malfunctions.
- Schedule regular pest control.
- In areas where rodents and pests are a problem, regularly check property for points of entry and plug those areas. This procedure is sometimes included in pest control contracts, but it's your responsibility to make sure it's being done.
- Schedule regular landscape maintenance and snow removal where applicable.

- Schedule regular carpet cleaning. Consider installing ceramic, hardwood, or solid surface flooring to replace the carpet.
- Schedule a deep cleaning at least once a year. This includes washing windows, throw rugs, curtains and blinds, ovens, baseboards, steam-cleaning sofas, etc.
- Wash all blankets and comforters at least once every ten rentals.
- Replace things before they get worn out and dingy, especially coffeemakers, toasters, blenders, towels, washcloths, pillows, curtains, and all bedding.
- Set up storm policies with your cleaning and maintenance people. Have them do whatever is necessary to storm-proof your property (e.g., pull patio furniture inside the house, turn off appliances, and so on).
- For owners who close their property for the winter, schedule your cleaning and maintenance people to check up on your property regularly during the closed season.

SUPPLIES ON HAND

This story demonstrates the importance of providing supplies for your renters. While at my condo in Florida one summer, my son came bursting in the door and shouted, "Mom, my teacher is here!" We happened to be vacationing in the same place at the same time. So I went out and began talking to her. After a while, she said, "Christine, can I ask you a favor? Can I borrow your broom?" She was renting a place on the beach that didn't have a broom! How could she possibly keep it clean while staying there? Think of all the sand that gets in! What an astonishing oversight on the owners' part!

Be sure to have these items on hand in your vacation rental property:

- Broom, mop, and vacuum
- Cleaning supplies, including window cleaner and bleach or disinfectant
- Plunger near each toilet
- Shovel and ice melt, sand, or salt
- Spackle and trowel
- Touch-up paint in a small jar that's clearly marked, paintbrush, or disposable sponge brush
- Hammer, screwdriver (flathead and Phillips), nails and screws, pliers, channel locks, and crescent wrench (found at hardware stores and dollar stores)
- Teflon tape for quick plumbing repairs
- A tube of silicone
- Wood glue
- Liquid drain opener (keep out of children's reach)
- Extra furnace filters
- Extra batteries for smoke detectors and TV remotes
- Lightbulbs in all sizes and wattages, including appliance bulbs
- Duct tape (there are millions of uses)

You can add many other items to this list, but I think you get the idea. Maintenance is not the nightmare subject you thought it was; things just don't go wrong that often—unless, of course, you don't prepare for it.

CLOSING FOR THE SEASON

A lot of property owners who face this situation ask, "Is it safe to lock up the place for the off-season?" To answer that question, first do some research. Most police departments provide statistics on crime in the area. Through the nonemergency number, call local police officers and talk with them about your concerns. Discuss the probability of your home being broken into and ask their advice to prevent break-ins and vandalism.

As another precaution, employ your cleaning person or other maintenance staff members to check on your place periodically throughout the "closed" season. Paying them a fee is likely less expensive and comes with fewer hassles than installing a security system.

Wildlife can be a much bigger problem than criminals when it comes to protecting places that are closed for the off-season. Critters are more apt to get in and do damage than are people. In my area of the country, raccoons are the first culprits that come to mind.

The Smiths opened their place in the spring to find it had been completely ransacked: cupboards opened, food spilled, beds unmade, sofa cushions torn apart, and more. They immediately called the police. Curiously, there was no sign of a break-in anywhere. After they cleaned up and went to bed that night, the culprits showed themselves. A whole family of raccoons, babies and all, had taken refuge in their house all winter long.

I suggest you spend more time and effort pest-proofing your place against raccoons, bears, mice, and other animals than worrying about vandals in the neighborhood.

When deciding to close for a season, consider special events that might warrant your staying open. If your vacation property is in an area that's actively boosting year-round tourism, capitalize on it. For instance, Skaneateles, New York, in the Finger Lakes region of upstate New York, is mostly a summer rental season. Yet, during the winter it has a monthlong Dickens village reenactment. This would be a perfect reason to keep your place open for rentals.

FURNISHING YOUR PLACE

Why do people rent vacation homes rather than just stay in a hotel? Convenience and comfort are big reasons. Not only will they have a kitchen, but they'll also have furnishings and other amenities that aren't found in a standard hotel room. They'll simply feel more at home.

Therefore, how you furnish your vacation home makes a big difference to your guests. It could even be a critical factor in their decision to return and in telling their friends what a gem they've found.

Kitchenware

Renters find nothing more annoying than cooking in an ill-equipped kitchen. By contrast, I can't tell you how many times my guests have complimented me on my well-equipped kitchen. When furnishing your kitchen, be sure to have ample supplies on hand. The rule of thumb is to have at least double the number of dishes, cups, glasses, and so on that your property sleeps. That is, if you sleep 8 people, then have enough supplies for 16. Why double up? First, because renters find having extras is convenient, especially while on vacation. People don't like having to take dirty dishes they used for breakfast out of the dishwasher and hand-wash them before lunch. That's work!

Second, having enough dishes and utensils helps conserve water and power. Then renters will only run the dishwasher because it's full, not because they need a clean plate.

Also supply a set of dishwasher-safe hard plastic cups, especially if you have a pool or hot tub, in case renters want to take drinks poolside. They also appreciate little plastic cups, bowls, and plates for their children (and that helps prevent spills and breakage).

Don't overlook the utensils, gadgets, and appliances that are specifically known in the area. For example, if your property is on the beach, having a big lobster pot and lobster/crab crackers on hand is essential. And if it's in a cold climate, offering a Crock-Pot and recipes that go with it for making soups or stews would be appreciated.

Quality of Furnishings

Your furnishings, including the linens, should be appropriate to your property's use and rental price. That means don't put satin sheets in a cabin that's mainly rented by men's hunting groups, and don't use a plastic outdoor patio set as your dining room table in a place that rents for $3,000 a week. Be aware of the levels of comfort and furnishings that renters expect in specific markets and price points. Do your best to make your place homey and welcoming, not stuffy or sparse. To add a touch of humanity, I suggest displaying your family photos around the property to give a personalized feel. Incidentally, they can serve as a deterrent for damages and theft. A friend who stayed at my place told me she laid my photo flat because she felt as though I was watching her. My response? Good!

When you are purchasing furnishings, keep in mind that you're going to be renting this property, not furnishing the Taj Mahal. Spend your money wisely. Take into consideration that you'll need to replace furnishings more often than you do at home. I don't recommend buying the highest quality of furniture as you might for your permanent home. I recommend buying less expensive furniture but don't scrape the bottom of the barrel. Just plan on replacing major pieces regularly. You can spend $3,000 for a sofa that's high quality and looks good, or spend $1,000 for one that looks good but is only of decent quality. For the same amount of money, you can replace that sofa three times and keep your furnishings looking fresh.

With some items, of course, you're wise to purchase the best quality. Kitchen table and dining room chairs are the first pieces that come to mind. The first place I owned had nice-looking, medium-size, quality chairs, but I found that within a few years, most of them broke. Let's face it, some people are pretty heavy. I recommend only buying chairs (interior and exterior) that have a 300-pound capacity. Many styles of wrought iron interior dining sets are available these days, and I highly recommend them.

Don't Use Old Stuff

Some people make the mistake of putting all their old furniture from their home into their rental properties instead of buying new furnishings. Your renters won't necessarily want that old stuff, either. So consider bringing old furniture to your local charity and take the tax write-off instead. I have used an occasional old piece of furniture here and there, but never without refinishing it or giving it a new coat of paint or faux finish.

I don't recommend filling your house with your treasured family heirlooms, either. Don't put items of value in your property that you'll worry about. I do recommend purchasing glass to cover the tops of wooden dining room and bedside tables, since people might forget to put coasters under their frosty glasses of lemonade.

As for beds in your home, make sure they're firm or extra firm. Comfortable beds are extremely important, as is the size. Indeed, having comfortable beds makes the difference between people coming back or not. The number one complaint to hotel staff is putting up with uncomfortable beds.

Renters don't want to compromise their preferred bed size, either. Ask any hotel clerk which rooms fill up first. You guessed it—

the ones that have king-size beds. If your renters have a king-size bed at home, chances are they'll have a tough time sleeping on anything smaller. If the master bedroom is not big enough for a king-size bed, then a queen-size bed should be adequate, but avoid a full-size bed. It simply doesn't work for most couples because it's too small.

Beware of Overimproving

Be conscious of any temptation to overimprove or overfurnish your vacation property, unless competing for rentals in your area requires fancy furnishings.

Remember, whatever improvements you make should be decided based on the vacationers' perspective. For example, with a budget of $5,000, should you install granite countertops or a hot tub? Although both will improve the property's resale value, look at this choice from the renters' perspective. Granite countertops improve the aesthetics of the place but it's not something people look for specifically. Instead, having a hot tub would make a huge difference in their vacationing experience. It's amenities like this that attract renters.

The same principle holds true for decorating. For example, don't spend thousands of dollars on original artwork. The question to ask is not, "Will someone damage the artwork?" but "Will it help rent the property?"

Keep asking yourself this question: "On a limited budget and with limited time, what can I do to improve the appearance and 'rentability' of this property?" What cosmetic things can be easily changed to create a welcoming sight when renters first walk in? An expensive sofa with a tropical flower print will stand out like a sore thumb in a cabin with rustic decor. A goal of good aesthetics would behoove you to change that. As always, use your common sense.

The rustic cabins I purchased in Tennessee were built with gold fixtures: faucets, chandeliers, lights, and so on. While they stick out in the rustic cabins, replacing them would cost me more than $1,000—would it be worth it? My solution was simple: I bought a can of speckled spray paint and painted the fixtures, so now they look more like they belong and it only cost six dollars for the can of paint. That left me with money to purchase other things that would attract more renters.

Dingy Doesn't Fly

One criterion you should definitely pay attention to is dinginess. Do the curtains, bedcovers, and blinds look crumpled and dusty? If so, clean them or replace them to create a fresh, welcoming look that attracts vacationers and makes their stay more pleasant. Applying a fresh coat of paint is always worth the time and money, too. But again, there's no need to go overboard with cosmetic changes.

Decorating your second home can be a lot of fun. But consider these words of caution: It's easy to get caught up buying too much decor for your vacation home. Avoid creating clutter for two equally important reasons. First, your housekeeper will hate you (having to dust all that extra stuff). The second reason is your renters' first impression—it's very important. If your renters see a lot of stuff when they first walk in, they might think that the place is cluttered or not clean. Be sure to give the best first impression possible.

SAFETY FIRST

Think very carefully before putting out "extras" that can be hazardous to children. Trinkets like wooden model sailboats can be cute, but they're a temptation for little hands. When you decorate, keep in mind that children's curiosity will occupy the rooms. Glass-topped coffee tables are durable, but I shudder to think of the toddler who falls onto the corner of one. Be sure to add plug covers on outlets and safety locks on cabinets. I suggest providing a high chair and porta-crib for times when renters request them. Be careful when supplying any items for infants and small children, as baby items are the most frequently recalled product by manufacturers (mainly for safety issues). For that reason, I don't recommend supplying car seats for babies.

Safety Inspections

Did you know that some states require periodic safety inspections? Check with your state sales tax office to learn if a state safety inspection is required for your property. Even if it isn't subject to an inspection, be sure that you have working smoke detectors, carbon monoxide detectors, and fire extinguishers. Clearly post emergency information such as evacuation plans, poison control centers, nearest hospital, and so on. As an added safety measure, purchase automatic shutoff irons and coffeemakers. Provide a first aid kit and information that warns visitors about local wildlife dangers (raccoons, bears, snakes, jellyfish, ticks, etc.).

FURNISHING CHECKLISTS

Furnishing your property is a mix of the practical and the aesthetic. A little creativity goes a long way. Although you don't want to spend a fortune, clearly you want to create an atmosphere that's warm, inviting, and safe for your guests—and for yourself. Use these lists to determine what your vacation home needs for the comfort of your guests.

Highly Recommended

Electric Appliances
Automatic coffeemaker (auto shutoff)
Blender (glass carafe)
Toaster (wide slot)
Electric can opener
Mixer
Iron (auto shutoff)
Ironing board
Vacuum cleaner
Alarm clock/radio

Dinnerware
If your property accommodates:
4 – you should have a service for 8
6 – you should have a service for 12
8 – you should have a service for 16
10 – you should have a service for 20
16 – you should have a service for 32

Dinner plates
Sandwich/salad plates
Cereal/soup bowls
Coffee cups/mugs
Serving bowls
Serving platters
Creamer
Sugar bowl with cover
Salt and pepper shakers

Flatware
Dinner forks
Salad forks
Tablespoons
Teaspoons
Table knives
Serving spoons

Glassware (tempered)
Tea glasses
Water glasses
Rocks glasses
Wineglasses

Cookware
Cookie sheet
Covered casserole
Medium covered saucepan
Medium skillet
13 × 9 baking dish
2 cake pans
2-quart Pyrex dish
3-piece mixing bowl set
Dutch oven w/lid
Hot pad/trivet
Large skillet
Large covered saucepan
Large glass casserole dish
Lobster pot
Muffin pan
Roaster with lid
Omelet pan
Tea kettle

Knives

Steak knives
3-inch paring knife
8-inch slicing knife
Chef's knife
Bread knife
Carving knife

Other kitchen items

Basting spoon
Broom/mop/dustpan
Butter dish
Can opener (manual)
Can piercer/bottle opener
Coasters/place mats
Colander
Corkscrew
Cutting board
Drying rack
Grater
Measuring cup
Measuring spoons
Meat fork
Micro/refrigerator dishes
Plastic pitcher
Potato masher
Rubber spatula
Salad bowl and serving spoons
Slotted spoon
Soup ladle
Spatula
Tongs
Vegetable peeler

Safety items

Fire extinguisher
First aid kit
Flashlight
Emergency candles
Matches
Smoke detectors
Plug covers
Safety locks for cabinets
Rubber tub mat

Linens

Sheets
Pillowcases
Pillow protectors
Pillows (2 per bed, including sofa bed)
Blankets
Bedspreads/comforters
Bath towels
Hand towels
Washcloths
Kitchen towels
Bath mat
Pot holder/oven mitt

Miscellaneous

Ashtrays (if applicable)
CD player
Family photos
Flyswatter
Hangers
Ice bucket
Lamps
Mattress pads

Miscellaneous continued

Phone/phone book

Plunger

Shower liner

TV (cable-ready with remotes)

VCR/DVD player

Waste cans

Add-on Amenities

Basketball hoop

BBQ grill and utensils

Beach chairs

Bikes

Boogie boards

Clothes-drying rack

Cookbooks

Crab/nut crackers

Crock-Pot

Dishwasher-safe plastic cups

Dog bowls

Doormats

Espresso maker

Fondue set

Games (Yahtzee, Scrabble, cards)

Hair dryer

Hatchet

High chair

Hot tub

Ice-cream scoop

Laundry basket

Napkin holder

Office tools (PC/printer/fax, ideally with
   high-speed Internet access)

Patio set

Plastic plates, cups, bowls for children

Porta-crib

Reading lamps

Rolling pin

Tennis racquets

Videos/DVDs

Volleyball net

Waffle iron

BEYOND FURNISHINGS

Besides furnishing your vacation home with obvious items that renters expect, add things that will make your place more enjoyable and show that you've put a lot of personal attention into it. I'm a true believer that every vacation property needs to have relaxing family activities on hand. These include movie videos, DVDs, music CDs, books, magazines, and games (having Yahtzee, Scrabble, and a deck or two of playing cards on hand are a must). If yours is a beach property, provide sand buckets and sand shovels. This stops the visiting kids from using your kitchen utensils as digging tools!

Also include various grooming items for the bathroom: blow-dryers, shampoo, soap, razors, and so on. If your property is in a ski resort, purchase extra hats and mittens from the dollar store. They'll be greatly appreciated by any skiers who lose theirs on the slopes.

When you buy these "extras," do people steal them? For the most part, no. But don't spend thousands of dollars filling your place with highly tempting items, either. Sometimes people take things home but, believe it or not, often they mail them back or they call and say, "We took these mitts home by mistake." People show much more honesty than you might expect.

Create a Personal Guidebook

Here's a bonus that's highly appreciated by guests. I create my own guidebook. I start with a three-ring binder filled with blank clear plastic sleeves. In the guidebook, I include notes about my property—where things can be found and how they work. I put in manuals for the stereo, VCR, and DVD player. And I spell out my checkout policies and "rules" for guests in this comprehensive book. It has saved a lot of searching time for my renters.

The fun part about putting it together is that I also fill my guidebook with information about area attractions, restaurant menus, church schedules, directions to grocery stores, and coupons. Here's an example of tips I created for renters in my Destin property:

D e s t i n   V a c a t i o n   T i p s

- *When you go to the outlet mall, stop first at the mall office, open until 6:30 PM (located behind the mall, accessible from Morgan's). Ask for a booklet called the Passport Book that's full of all sorts of coupons for most of the stores . . . also if the men decide to go shopping too and get tired, the mall has a billiard room above the food court. If you take the kids along, Morgan's also has a game room. In the Passport Book, look for a coupon to buy $5 worth of tokens and get $5 free.*
- *Deep-sea fishing is great in Destin. If the guys like deep-sea fishing, this is a must for them.*
- *Seaside is a nice little village east down Highway 98 (watch for the signs, you'll take a right). Seaside is a very upscale area that's fun to visit and dream about when you win the lottery. It has a bunch of artsy shops. Even though things are very expensive, it's a fun place to look around.*
- *Keep your eyes open. On the beach at dusk or dawn, we very often see dolphins swimming right off shore. If the dolphins come in close, which they do occasionally, don't get in the water or try to touch them. Please respect that they are wildlife. In fact, it's illegal to touch the dolphins (humans carry germs that harm them).*
- *A fun, cheap thing to do is to rent the ocean kayaks off the beach. Morning is usually the best time, when the waters are generally calm. The kayaks are very easy to maneuver and only cost about $10/hour to rent.*
- *There are a lot of great restaurants in the area. The Back Porch in Destin is one of our favorites. Depending on the season, it can be very crowded, so be prepared to wait. It has a playground on the beach for the kids to play at while waiting. I recommend you bring a change of clothes for the little ones; it's tough to resist the temptation when playing near the water and it's better to be prepared than to get upset when they inevitably get wet. Remember you're on vacation!*
- *If you want to cook a seafood feast, my favorite store is called Shrimpers. To get there, go east on Highway 98, past the outlet mall about*

six or eight miles. It's on the lefthand side, past Bayou Bill's. Shrimpers has the freshest fish and shrimp and great prices. A local specialty is the smoked tuna dip–great on crackers as an appetizer. Also, if you can get your hands on red shrimp, they're a must-try! Boil them in water for 1½ minutes (no more, no less!), and them dip them in drawn butter. You'll think you're eating lobster. Typically reds are only available on Tuesdays. Shrimpers also has the best key lime pie around!

- *Another seafood market, Destin Ice, has a full-time chef prepare things that you can cook at home. It's supposed to simplify making "home-cooked gourmet food." It's located on Highway 98 to the west, on the right, almost all the way down to the bridge to the island.*

- *I've discovered a new dollar store on Highway 98 that has a lot of useful items, all for $1. It's a great place to pick up odds and ends you forgot to pack. It's located west of the condo just pass the Home Depot on the right.*

- *There can be some ocean-related deaths along the Gulf Coast. Please pay attention to the flags on the beach. If there is a red flag, do not swim. The riptides (rip currents) can be very strong. If you get caught in a riptide, swim parallel to the beach until you are out of it, then swim to shore. Maravilla Beach does not have lifeguards.*

SET ASIDE A CLOSET FOR YOU

By the way, don't forget your own needs! You need a place to store personal things that you don't want your renters to have access to. So designate a closet for items you own and lock it.

In the vacation home where my family goes, I keep all our personal belongings in one closet so we can easily pack up and leave at the end of our time there. Specifically, I put all of our toiletries, personal bedding (I like my own), laundry detergent, cleaning supplies, and extra supplies for my property in this closet. I even keep some nonperishable food items there. I always keep this closet locked, though my cleaning staff has a key to it, just in case something is urgently needed.

Many owners are reluctant to remove the use of a closet from a bedroom. Don't be. I took a closet from the smallest bedroom in one of our properties, converted it into our owner's closet, then purchased a wardrobe at an estate sale and placed it right in front of the closet door. This way, my renters still have a place to hang their things and all my belongings are stashed away, out of sight.

Remember, the goal is to make owning this vacation home as easy and convenient as possible for you, too. After all, enjoying it is the real reason you bought this vacation home in the first place.

12

BEING A GOOD NEIGHBOR (FROM AFAR)

It's easy to overlook the value of networking with your vacation property neighbors. When owning a second home from a distance, you're wise to collaborate in many ways for many reasons—well beyond borrowing a cup of sugar. It's not only important to get to know your neighbors—it's also vital! Here are several reasons why.

REFERRED BOOKINGS

Time and again, when I've already booked my properties, I can refer potential vacationers to a neighbor's property with a hearty recommendation. After all, people always feel more comfortable dealing with someone who comes recommended. In my experience, a high percentage of referred vacation rentals get booked after receiving a referral from another human being. There's simply an increased level of comfort. I've had several opportunities to refer callers to my neighbors' vacation homes. And because I've seen the properties, I can help answer questions.

Another reason to know your neighbors is they can help you close the deal on inquiries to rent your place. Often, renters who book one of my properties want to know about other properties nearby because several families are vacationing together. Many times, they'll rent mine if there are neighboring properties available. Passing on a phone number so they can check into renting my neighbor's vacation home represents another golden opportunity for a quick booking.

Piggyback Marketing

When you get to know your vacation home neighbors, you also can piggyback on each other's marketing efforts (if you've already agreed to pass on referrals). For example, I might have my properties listed on five Web sites, and my neighbor has hers listed on five sites, but there are only two that we both list on. Together, we've just expanded our marketing reach at no extra cost.

I suggest that you don't look at referring potential customers to neighboring owners as competition. I've found that when I forward bookings to other owners, they inevitably come back to me at some point in time. Cooperating on bookings in this business goes a long way. Besides, it's the neighborly thing to do!

SHARED MAINTENANCE

Think about the benefits of collaborating on maintenance issues with a fellow owner, as noted in Chapter 11. You can pool your resources and find maintenance people and/or housekeepers, who you can hire collectively. Here's a story of why it's beneficial to get to know some of your neighbors.

Dianne and I have each owned a condo in the same building for over seven years. Whenever Dianne goes to Florida, she checks on my condo, and when I go, I do the same for her. We've collaborated and had

many maintenance projects done to our properties with the same con-
tractors at the same time. Sometimes I oversee the work, and sometimes
she oversees it. We both visit our places two or three times a year. Inter-
estingly, in the seven years of ownership, we've never been there at the
same time. While hard to believe, it's great for our properties. This way
they get visited and checked on four to six times a year.

HOW TO FIND YOUR NEXT-DOOR NEIGHBOR

How many times have you borrowed things and shared ideas
with your neighbors at home? In your vacation home community,
the same dynamic happens. You can bounce ideas off one another and help each other. In fact, you might have more things in
common with your vacation home neighbors than with your
neighbors at home because you're in the same business. Even if
your neighbor uses a management company, you'll still need
many of the same things. It's no coincidence that I mention the
value of networking throughout this book—it's vital.

It's generally easy to find out who other owners are—you'll
meet each other when you visit your properties. If your vacation
home is part of an association, you can obtain a list of owners directly from the association. When the association holds its annual
homeowners meeting, take time to socialize with your fellow owners. Try to find owners who live in your hometown. This can be
especially helpful when you want to transport small items and
supplies to your property.

You also may be able to find other owners from their management companies, although don't expect the representatives to
give out their names and numbers. Instead, ask if they would contact other owners on your behalf and have them call you.

You can even ask current renters directly. Don't be shy. When
you see them, strike up a conversation. These guests might know
the owners themselves. Or they might *be* the owners. The point is,
find out who your neighbors are and get to know them.

Attend Seminars

Another great way to meet owners like you is by attending a seminar designed for vacation home owners. The seminars I give to owners and prospective owners provide golden opportunities to network. (For a list of upcoming seminar locations and lots of useful information, go to my Web site at http://www.HowToRent ByOwner.com.)

Beyond all the information property owners learn at my seminars, they also enjoy seeing and meeting other owners in their communities. They value the camaraderie and feel more comfortable knowing other property owners they can turn to in case of need. A lot of friendships have been formed at my seminars—and also a lot of deals.

Networking in Cyberspace

A monitored chat group for vacation rental owners was started in 2003 through Yahoo! This group has made it easy to build an owners community in cyberspace. By joining the 1,500+ members of this online group, you can glean lots of advice from owners who have dealt with similar problems you might be experiencing. Owners who once e-mailed me directly with their questions now seek advice from participants in this group through daily postings. After all, I haven't experienced every single situation that comes up—far from it. So by sending questions to the group, owners get answers and opinions quickly from various points of view, not just mine.

It's clear to see you help other owners without the express purpose of getting something back—it's simply the right thing to do. And because what goes around comes around, you'll likely find other owners will do the same for you.

BEING INVOLVED IN HOMEOWNERS ASSOCIATIONS (HOAS)

Officers in homeowners associations are responsible for maintenance, upkeep, and financial management of common areas in complexes and neighborhoods where you own property.

Being involved in any organization generally means more than participating in the financial aspects. Becoming an active member of your association from afar isn't as difficult as you might think. Many people believe that since they live a distance from their second homes, it would be impossible to be an active member of their HOA. Chances are, many of the owners also live far away. Most HOAs hold open meetings quarterly or annually. Often, an HOA board needs input and opinions from many owners.

Why Get Involved

I'm a firm believer in community involvement; if you're not involved, you have no right to complain.

- Don't sit back and expect someone else to do your job for you.
- Reap the benefits and rewards of a well-run association, which in the long run is maintaining or improving your property value.
- Meet other owners.

What You Can Do

- You can easily arrange your maintenance visit to your property to coincide with the timing of association meetings.
- You can volunteer to handle small tasks that can be done remotely, like coordinating association newsletters or compiling directories.

- Maybe you can volunteer to organize a social event or research items to be purchased or new maintenance service providers (such as a landscaper, pool service, etc.). These tasks don't require you to be at a board meeting every month.

Homeowners associations' biggest gripe of all is not enough people having sent in their proxies, so they don't have a quorum when they have something they have to vote on. Some association bylaws specify very strict guidelines concerning what needs to be approved by the board and what requires a quorum. If an HOA board can't get the quorum to vote, its hands are tied.

The main reason people don't send in their proxies is because they are not familiar with the board member candidates. I think it's better to vote for someone you don't know than not vote at all. Again, not having a quorum can tie the board's hands.

Remember the saying: Ten percent of the people do 100 percent of the work? A homeowners association wouldn't be so much of a burden to a few if everyone took some time to be responsible for some of the tasks. Get involved!

Zo's Ski Resort Home

Zo and his wife own property in a popular Colorado ski resort, a two-hour drive from where they live. They purchased it 16 years ago and rent it 10 to 16 weeks a year. The good news is they're able to use their property a whopping 60 nights a year themselves!

Renting in the ski area, they quickly discovered that all their renters expect to enjoy access to a hot tub, so Zo got involved in the homeowners association. He took time to get to know the association leaders and persuaded them of the importance of building a hot tub on the premises—for the benefit of residents and rental guests alike. Before long, it proved to be a wise investment that made a difference in attracting renters as well as getting to know his neighbors.

Chapter

13

FINAL NOTES FROM
THE AUTHOR

Think of this not as the end of the book,
but rather as the start of a new adventure.

You have just finished reading this book
and have a lot of information to digest. Right now, take some
time to process the key ideas addressed here:

- What kind of second home or vacation property is right for
  you?
- Who needs to be on your team to find a property, finance
  it, inspect it, insure it, manage it, clean it, and maintain it?
- What can you hope to gain for yourself? For your family?
  For your financial future?
- Does owning a second home as a vacation rental make
  sense for you?

I remember when my husband and I bought our first vacation
property, we really couldn't afford it. We felt overwhelmed with
all the logistics of purchasing, owning, and renting our vacation
home. But we did a lot of research and our adventure worked out

much better than we'd ever imagined. We're definitely happy we took the plunge.

You can either talk yourself right out of buying a vacation home or you can choose to take the risk.

40 YEARS FROM NOW

Let me share some words of wisdom from a vacation rental property owner who has been at this much longer than myself—in fact, for 40 years. He said, "I bought a house on Hawaii in 1965 for about $25,000. My wife wanted to sell it when we left there in 1971. At that time, we could have sold it for about $75,000 (triple the price in six years). My opinion prevailed. This house is now worth about $1 million. That's 40 times the original value (except it's really only 20 times because we had to pay another $25,000 to buy the land). Forty years later, we're sitting in that house in Hawaii."

Your question: Where should we invest? My answer: Anywhere you would like to be sitting, many years from now, retired, with all your mortgage and expenses paid through rental income.

INSPIRED!

Let me close with my favorite article that continually inspires me. I read it as if it were poetry. In it, I find many underlying hidden messages pertaining to all aspects of owning and managing properties. Read it. And then take the risk!

OF RISK AND REWARD

by Jack Simpson, Real Estate Broker, Columnist, and Vacation Home Owner

Life is richer and more rewarding for those who take risks to get what they want. Most all truly great achievements involve risk. This applies in the various fields of exploration, competitive sports, business, finance, even love and war. Real estate investing is no exception.

In the course of my business, I meet a lot of people who are looking for something more out of life. For many of them, it's a vacation rental home at the beach. The rewards are there to be had: pride of ownership, free personal use, rental income, and good potential for appreciation. But there are risks, too. What if it doesn't rent? What if there's a hurricane? What of the unknown? Most bold, self-confident people go for it all—the risk and the reward. They buy. The timid talk themselves out of it. I feel sorry for them.

I am accustomed to taking risks, not only in real estate investing but in many other facets of life. If I see something I want, I go for it. Sometimes I hit. Sometimes I miss. But at least I am in there swinging. I have learned to savor the success and learn from the ones that don't work out. Along this line, I have some thoughts to share with you.

Control the risk. You can exert control over certain activities such as selecting your own investments or managing your own business. But you have absolutely no control over the spin of a roulette wheel or the draw of the lottery. I take risks but I don't gamble. There's a big difference.

Enjoy the risk. That's right—enjoy it. Risk is a challenge. It excites and sharpens the senses. Most people perform better under pressure. Some thrive on it. Who would play a golf course if it had no sand traps or water hazards? A world without challenge would be downright depressing.

Concentrate on your goal. Don't be distracted by obstacles and negative thoughts. Think about the golf course. You don't hit a hole in one if all you can think about is staying out of the rough. Whether you expect to win or to lose, you are probably right.

Accept all setbacks. Not every venture will be successful, but that doesn't mean it failed either. You fail only if you stop trying. Almost every success story is full of setbacks along the way. They build character and make you a strong person.

Consider the alternative. Trying to eliminate the risks often creates other risks. Some people put all their money in a "safe" insured account only to see their buying power taken away by taxes and inflation. Ask yourself, "What's the worst that can happen?" To me, the worst thing is seeing your life slip by without the risk and reward. That's sad.

We have all heard "Nothing ventured, nothing gained," and "Better to have loved and lost . . . ," and those saddest of words ". . . it might have been." But I believe Kris Kristofferson put it best when he wrote the song "I'd rather be sorry for something I've done than for something I didn't do."

A

FORMS FOR RENT-BY-OWNER PROPERTIES

This book makes reference to proper documentation and forms, which are important for both you and your renters to have to make your business run smoothly. The sample forms included here are:

- Confirmation of Booking
- Directions and Arrival Policy, Departure Information, Emergency Information
- Rules and Regulations (Cabin)
- Rules and Regulations (Beach home)
- Deposit Refund Letter
- Pet Policy

I recommend that you build a template for these forms in your word-processing program. This can be accomplished by using popular programs such as Microsoft Word or Word Perfect. Save these templates and use them again and again. All of these forms can be e-mailed directly to your guests except for the deposit refund, which you would mail with your deposit refund check. However, I don't recommend that you e-mail them as attachments. Recipients may not have a compatible program to open attachments and/or they may be reluctant to open them because of Internet viruses. Simply copy these forms into the body of the e-mail.

To convert your documents from your word processor to your e-mail using Windows on a PC: Open your word-processing document template. Fill in the necessary information (i.e., today's date, names, dates of rental, etc.), then select the whole document (Ctrl-A) and use your copy command (Ctrl-C). Next, open an e-mail document and put your cursor over the body of the message. Now press your paste command (Ctrl-V). Simple, isn't it?

Here are some sample documents that you can customize to suit your property. I suggest you have an attorney look over your forms to make sure the wording complies with the law.

CONFIRMATION OF BOOKING

E-mail this form to your prospective renters at the time they book your vacation home. Do not send them as attachments. Remember, do not accept a payment without having this form signed and returned to you.

CONFIRMATION OF BOOKING

Enclosed is our rental contract and rules. Please print, read, and sign and send it along with your $200 deposit to the address below. Thanks so much. If you have any questions, feel free to contact me.

Mr. and Mrs. Owner

Your name
Your address
Your city, state, and zip
Your phone number
Your e-mail
Your Web site

January 25, 2005

Dear Mr. and Mrs. Guest,

Thank you for choosing our condominium for your vacation. We hope that you have a pleasant stay. The unit is located in the My Resort complex at 4567 Scenic Drive, Destin, FL 32541, Unit #1234, Phone 850-654-3210.

Your confirmation is as follows:

Check-in date: June 19, 2005, after 3 PM CST (No early check-in please)
Checkout date: June 26, 2005, by 10 AM CST
Number of people in party: 2 adults, 2 children

After I receive your $200 deposit, your bill is as follows:

Total bill $1,581.75 = $1,350.00 (rental rate) + $75.00 (cleaning fee) + $156.75 (11% Florida tax)
1st payment of $790.87 due April 19, 2005 (60 days prior)
2nd payment of $790.88 due June 5, 2005 (14 days prior)

As soon as I receive your final payment, I will send/call the lockbox/key instructions. Please sign and return 1 copy of this confirmation and 1 copy of the rules.

Thanks! Have a great vacation!

Mr. and Mrs. Owner

Signature _____ Date _____

DIRECTIONS AND ARRIVAL POLICY, DEPARTURE INFORMATION, EMERGENCY INFORMATION

Send these forms as one document to your renters only *after* you receive final payment. Be sure to have all the following information both on your directions to renters and posted in your property.

In addition to e-mailing the emergency information to guests with the other documents, I suggest you copy this information on pretty paper, frame it, and place it near the telephone in the property.

Directions and Arrival Policy

I received your final payment. Thanks! Enclosed are all the directions you will need to get into the condo. Have a great time, Christine

Directions to My Resort complex: *Give clear directions from all points, north, south, east, west, airport, etc. Be sure to include landmarks before and after (in case they passed it) your property.*

My Resort Complex is located at 4567 Scenic Drive, Destin, FL 32541, Unit #1234. The resort is located east of Destin (proper). It is between the Wal-Mart and the Silver Sands Outlet Mall.

There is an entrance into My Resort complex from the main road through Destin, Hwy. 98, or you can access the resort from Scenic Drive. The security gate code is 123456.

Coming from the Airport, take a left out of the airport, go to the end of the road and turn left onto State Rt. 31. Once you pass the Burger King, take a right onto the Mid-Bay Bridge (toll road $2); at the end of the bridge, take a left and follow the directions coming from west.

Coming from the west, you'll pass Wal-Mart (on left) and Home Depot (on left). After signs for Miramar Beach watch for the My Resort complex sign on the right. If you get to the Silver Sands Outlet Mall, you've gone too far. Once in the complex, take your first right, then proceed to the condo buildings.

Coming from the east, you'll pass Sandestin, then turn Left at the first sign for the beaches onto Scenic Drive (Silver Sands Outlet Mall on right). Stay on Scenic Drive, approximately 2 miles. My Resort complex will be on the right (just past Neighbor).

Once in My Resort, proceed to Condo Bldg #1. We're unit #1234 (second floor).

The lockbox code is 01234, take the keys out; keep them with you at all times. When you leave, **PLEASE leave the keys on the kitchen table.** No early check-in is allowed. Beach gate code is 9876.

When you arrive, please inspect the condo for cleanliness; if ANYTHING is not acceptable, do not hesitate to call the housekeeper, Mrs. Clean, at 850-987-6543 (home) or 850-876-5432 (cell).

Thanks and have a great vacation!

Departure Information

Before leaving the condo, please be sure to do the following:

- Take out all trash to the dumpster.
- Load and run the dishwasher.
- Leave the keys on the kitchen table. (Lock the door with the doorknob lock.)
- Leave by 10 AM.
- Sign our guest book.

Have a safe journey home.

Emergency Information

In case of emergency, dial **911.**
Poison Control: 850-654-3219
    You are in Walton County
    My Resort, in Destin, Florida
Address is:
    4567 Scenic Drive,
    Destin, FL 32541
    Unit #1234
    Phone 850-654-3210

If you have trouble with the property, call Mr. and Mrs. Owner. Call collect, 777-123-4567.

We can also be reached on our cell phone at 888-123-4567.

If you cannot reach us, please call the housekeeper, Mrs. Clean, at 850-987-6543 (home) or 850-876-5432 (cell).

RULES AND REGULATIONS

E-mail these rules to your renters at the time of booking. Do not send them as attachments. *Remember, do not accept a payment without receiving this form back from the renters.*

RULES AND REGULATIONS (Cabin)

The cabin is located at 1234 Mountain Road, Sevierville, TN 37862, Phone 000-123-4567.

1. **CHECK-IN TIME** IS AFTER 3 PM EST AND **CHECKOUT** IS 10 AM EST. NO early check-ins.
2. This is a **NONSMOKING** cabin.
3. **Pets are permitted** in rental cabins only with prior approval. $50 per pet fee applies. All pets must be leashed at all times. Pet owners are responsible for cleaning up any/all pet refuse. Pets are not allowed on furniture at any time. Any evidence of pets on furniture may incur extra cleaning fees. All pets must be up-to-date on rabies vaccinations and all other vaccinations. Heartworm preventative is highly recommended. All pets are to be treated with Advantage or similar topical flea and tick repellent three (3) days prior to arrival. Fleas and ticks are very rampant in this area and can cause harmful/fatal illness to humans and pets. All items above are the sole responsibility of the pet owner. The cabin owners assume no responsibility for illness or injury that may incur to pets or humans while on the premises.
4. We will not rent to vacationing **students or singles under 25** years of age unless accompanied by an adult guardian or parent.
5. **DAMAGE/RESERVATION DEPOSIT**—A damage/reservation deposit of $200 is required. This must be received within five (5) days of booking the reservation. The deposit automatically converts to a security/damage deposit upon arrival. The deposit is NOT applied toward rent; however, it is fully refundable within fourteen (14) days of departure, provided the following provisions are met:
   • No damage is done to the cabin or its contents, beyond normal wear and tear.

- No charges are incurred due to contraband, pets, or collection of rents or services rendered during the stay.
- All debris, rubbish, and discards are placed in refuse containers outside, and soiled dishes are placed in the dishwasher and cleaned. One load of laundry is started.
- All keys are left in the lockbox and cabin is left locked.
- All charges accrued during the stay are paid prior to departure.
- No linens are lost or damaged.
- NO early check-in or late checkout.

---

1. **PAYMENT**—An advance payment equal to 50% of the rental rate is required 60 days before arrival. The advance payment will be applied toward the room rent. Please make payments in the form of traveler's checks, bank money orders, cashier's checks, or personal checks payable to Christine Karpinski. The advance payment is not a damage deposit. The BALANCE OF RENT is due fourteen (14) days before your arrival date.

2. **CANCELLATIONS**—A sixty (60) day notice is required for cancellation. Cancellations that are made more than sixty (60) days prior to the arrival date will incur no penalty except if deposits were made via credit card. All credit card cancellations are subject to a 5% cancellation fee or $50 whichever is greater. Cancellations or changes that result in a shortened stay, that are made within 60 days of the arrival date, forfeit the full advance payment and damage/reservation deposit. Cancellation or early departure does not warrant any refund of rent or deposit.

3. **MONTHLY RESERVATION CANCELLATIONS**—Monthly renters must cancel one hundred twenty (120) days prior to check-in. Monthly renters who make a change that results in a shortened stay must cancel at least ninety (90) days prior to check-in.

4. **MAXIMUM OCCUPANCY**—The maximum number of guests per cabin is limited to six (6) persons. An additional charge of $10 per person per night for guests in addition to six (6) will be assessed. THIS PROPERTY REQUIRES A THREE (3) NIGHT MINIMUM STAY; four (4) nights during peak and holiday seasons.

5. Longer **minimum stays** may be required during holiday periods. If a rental is taken for less than three days, the guest will be charged the three-night rate.

6. **INCLUSIVE FEES**—Rates include a one-time linen-towel setup. Amenity fees are included in the rental rate.

7. **NO DAILY CLEANING SERVICE**—While linens and bath towels are included in the cabin, daily cleaning service is not included in the rental rate; however, it is available at an additional rate. We suggest you bring your own beach towels. We do not permit towels or linens to be taken from the cabins.

8. **RATE CHANGES**—Rates subject to change without notice.

9. **FALSIFIED RESERVATIONS**—Any reservation obtained under false pretense will be subject to forfeiture of advance payment, deposit, and/or rental money, and the party will not be permitted to check in.

10. **WRITTEN EXCEPTIONS**—Any exceptions to the above-mentioned policies must be approved in writing in advance.

11. **PARKING**—Parking is limited to two (2) vehicles. Vehicles are to be parked in designated parking areas only. Parking on the road is not permitted. Any illegally parked cars are subject to towing and applicable fines/towing fees and are the sole responsibility of the vehicle owner.

12. **HOT TUBS**—No children under the age of 12 permitted in hot tubs at any time. When using the hot tub, remember there is a certain health risk associated with this facility. Use at your own risk. Our housekeepers drain, sanitize, refill, and replenish chemicals in all hot tubs prior to your arrival; therefore, it may not be warm till later that evening. Hot tub covers are for insulation purposes and are not designed to support a person or persons. DO NOT STAND ON THE HOT TUB COVERS; they will break and you may be charged for replacement. Remember, when not using the hot tub, leave cover on so hot tub will stay warm.

13. **STORM POLICY/ROAD CONDITIONS**—No refunds will be given for storms. Mountain roads can be curvy and steep. Gravel drives are well maintained; however, we highly recommend four-wheel drive and/or chains during the snow months. We do not refund due to road conditions.

14. All of the cabins are privately owned; the owners are not responsible for any accidents, injuries, or illnesess that occur while on the premises or its facilities. The homeowners are not responsible for the loss of personal belongings or valuables of the guest. By accepting this reservation, it is agreed that all guests are expressly assuming the risk of any harm arising from their use of the premises or others who they invite to use the premises.

By signing below, I agree to all terms and conditions of this agreement.

Signature _____ Date _____

If you wish to use a credit card for this rental, please provide the following information:

Name as it appears on credit card:

_____

Credit card billing address:

_____

City _____ State _____ Zip Code _____

Type of credit card: MasterCard / Visa

Credit card number _____

Expiry date _____

I hereby give permission to charge my credit card for the amounts above. By signing below, I agree to all terms and conditions of this agreement.

Signature _____ Date _____

RULES AND REGULATIONS (Beach home)

My Resort complex
4567 Scenic Drive, Destin, FL 32541, Unit #1234, Phone 850-654-3210

1. **CHECK-IN TIME** IS AFTER 3 PM CST AND **CHECKOUT** IS 10 AM CST. NO early check-ins.
2. This is a **NONSMOKING** unit.
3. **Pets are not permitted** in rental units under any conditions.
4. We will not rent to vacationing **students or singles under 25** years of age unless accompanied by an adult guardian or parent.
5. **DAMAGE/RESERVATION DEPOSIT**—A damage/reservation deposit of $200 is required. This must be received within seven (7) days of booking the reservation. The deposit automatically converts to a security/damage deposit upon arrival. The deposit is NOT applied toward rent; however, it is fully refundable within fourteen (14) days of departure, provided the following provisions are met:

   • No damage is done to unit or its contents, beyond normal wear and tear.
   • No charges are incurred due to contraband, pets, or collection of rents or services rendered during the stay.
   • All debris, rubbish, and discards are placed in dumpster, and soiled dishes are placed in the dishwasher and cleaned.
   • All keys are left on the kitchen table and unit is left locked.
   • All charges accrued during the stay are paid prior to departure.
   • No linens are lost or damaged.
   • NO early check-in or late checkout.
   • Parking passes are left inside the unit upon departure.
   • The renter is not evicted by the owner (or representative of the owner), the local law enforcement, or the security company employed by My Resort complex.

1. **PAYMENT—**An advance payment equal to 50% of the rental rate is required sixty (60) days before arrival. The advance payment will be applied toward the room rent. Please make payments in the form of traveler's checks, bank money orders, cashier's checks, or personal checks payable to Christine Karpinski. The advance payment is not a damage deposit. The BALANCE OF RENT is due fourteen (14) days before your arrival date.

2. **CANCELLATIONS—**A sixty (60) day notice is required for cancellation. Cancellations that are made more than sixty (60) days prior to the arrival date will incur no penalty. Cancellations or changes that result in a shortened stay that are made within sixty (60) days of the arrival date forfeit the full advance payment and damage/reservation deposit. Cancellation or early departure does not warrant any refund of rent or deposit.

3. **MONTHLY RESERVATION CANCELLATIONS—**Monthly renters must cancel one hundred twenty (120) days prior to check-in. Monthly renters who make a change that results in a shortened stay must cancel at least ninety (90) days prior to check-in.

4. **MAXIMUM OCCUPANCY—**The maximum number of guests per condominium is limited to eight (8) persons. An additional charge of $10 per person per night for guests in addition to eight (8) will be assessed. THIS PROPERTY REQUIRES A THREE (3) NIGHT MINIMUM STAY.

5. Longer **minimum stays** may be required during holiday periods. If a rental is taken for less than three days, the guest will be charged the three-night rate.

6. **INCLUSIVE FEES—**Rates include a one-time linen-towel setup. Amenity fees are included in the rental rate.

7. **NO DAILY CLEANING SERVICE—**While linens and bath towels are included in the unit, daily cleaning service is not included in the rental rate; however, it is available at an additional rate. We suggest you bring beach towels. We do not permit towels or linens to be taken from the units.

8. **RATE CHANGES—**Rates subject to change without notice.

9. **FALSIFIED RESERVATIONS—**Any reservation obtained under false pretense will be subject to forfeiture of advance payment, deposit, and/or rental money, and the party will not be permitted to check in.

10. **WRITTEN EXCEPTIONS**—Any exceptions to the above-mentioned policies must be approved in writing in advance.
11. **PARKING PASSES**—Parking passes are located inside the unit. Renter must display parking pass on the rearview mirror at all times. Failure to display may result in towing of vehicle at renter's expense. Leave the parking passes inside the unit upon departure.
12. **HURRICANE OR STORM POLICY**—No refunds will be given unless:
    - The National Weather Service orders mandatory evacuations in a "Tropical Storm/Hurricane Warning" area and/or
    - A mandatory evacuation order has been given for the "Tropical Storm/Hurricane Warning" area of residence of a vacationing guest.

    The day that the National Weather Service orders a mandatory evacuation order in a "Tropical Storm/Hurricane Warning" area, we will refund:

    - Any unused portion of rent from a guest currently registered;
    - Any unused portion of rent from a guest who is scheduled to arrive and wants to shorten their stay to come in after the Hurricane Warning is lifted; and
    - Any advance rents collected or deposited for a reservation that is scheduled to arrive during the Hurricane Warning period.

By signing below, I agree to all terms and conditions of this agreement.

Signature _____ Date _____

If you wish to use a credit card for this rental, please provide the following information:

Name as it appears on credit card:

_____

Credit card billing address:

_____

City _____ State _____ Zip Code _____

Type of credit card: MasterCard / Visa

Credit card number _____

Expiry date _____

I hereby give permission to charge my credit card for the amounts above. By signing below, I agree to all terms and conditions of this agreement.

Signature _____ Date _____

DEPOSIT REFUND LETTER

Send this letter with the refund after you have confirmation from your housekeeper that there was no damage or theft.

Your name
Your address
Your city, state, zip code
Your phone number
Your e-mail address
Web page http://www.yourwebsiteaddress.com
Today's date

Dear Mr. and Mrs. Renter,

Thank you for choosing our condominium for your vacation. We hope that you had a pleasant stay. The condo was left in good condition; therefore, enclosed you'll find your $200 deposit refund.

If you wish to rent again, just call/e-mail me. I will start taking spring 2006 reservations in September 2005. I do book up quickly, so just keep that in mind if you're set on particular dates.

Looking forward to hearing from you again.

Thanks again!

Christine

PET POLICY

For a sample pet policy form, go to The Humane Society's Web site, http://www.hsus.org/ace/11803, or http://www.RentWithPets.org.

WEB SITES FOR ADVERTISING

PORTAL WEB SITES

Remember, I recommend you list your property on three to five Web sites. Below are Web sites that I consider the best in the industry.

Christine's Top Picks

http://www.CyberRentals.com

Established in June 1995, GreatRentals.com now advertises more than 17,000 properties for 12,000+ property owners worldwide.

http://www.GreatRentals.com

Established in March 1997, CyberRentals.com now advertises more than 9,300 properties for 6,200+ property owners worldwide.

http://www.Holiday-Rentals.com

Established in March 1996, Holiday-Rentals.com now advertises more than 10,000 properties in 60 countries for 6,700+ owners of vacation properties. It does not charge commission, just a fixed annual advertising fee.

http://www.VacationRentals.com

Established in 1997, VacationRentals.com has 14,300 listings, including 2,200 free trail listings. Listings are in 109 different countries around the world.

http://www.VacationVillas.net

Established in 1997, VacationVillas.net, and its German-speaking site FeWo-direkt.de, is by far the most popular and visited vacation rental index on the German-speaking Internet. It has more than 9,000 listings, mostly in Europe.

http://www.VRBO.com

Established in November 1995, Vacation Rentals by Owner® has more than 33,000 properties in 95 world areas, chiefly in the United States but also in 30 European countries and 30 Caribbean destinations.

Honorable Mentions

http://www.10kvacationrentals.com

http://www.cafegetaway.com

http://www.choice1.com

http://www.costaholidays.com

http://www.cottageportal.com

http://www.craigslist.org

http://www.goin2travel.com

http://www.greatrentals.com

http://www.gulfcoastrentals.com

http://www.holiday-rentals.uk.com

http://www.krazymoose.com

http://www.lakerentals.com

http://www.mountain-lodging.com

http://www.nyvacationrentals.com

http://www.ownerdirect.com

http://www.perfectplaces.com

http://www.rentalsinthepoconos.com

http://www.shorevacations.com

http://www.srbo.com

http://www.tropicrentals.com

http://www.vacationrentalspaces.com

http://www.vacationrentals411.com

VACATION EXCHANGE WEB SITES

Trade your vacation property with other owners around the world. They are listed here alphabetically.

http://www.blue-home.com

http://www.christianhomexchange.com

http://www.digsville.com

http://www.exchangehomes.com

http://www.exchangeplaces.com

http://www.homeexchange.com

http://www.homeinvite.com

http://www.seniorshomeexchange.com

http://www.sunswap.com

http://www.traveler-exchange.com

http://www.trading-homes.com

http://www.swapngo.co.uk

C

STATE SALES TAX OFFICES

This appendix provides contact information to learn about collecting and paying state sales tax on your vacation rental property.

Alabama
http://www.ador.state.al.us/salestax/index.html

Alaska
http://www.dced.state.ak.us/dca/LOGON/tax/tax-sales.htm

Arizona
http://www.revenue.state.az.us

Arkansas
http://www.state.ar.us/dfa/odd/salestax_index.html

California
http://www.boe.ca.gov/sutax/faqscont.htm

Colorado
http://www.revenue.state.co.us/TPS_Dir/wrap.asp?incl=salestaxforms

Connecticut
http://www.ct.gov

Delaware
http://www.state.de.us/revenue/index.htm

Florida
http://www.myflorida.com/dor/taxes/sales_tax.html

Georgia
http://www2.state.ga.us/departments/dor/salestax/index.shtml

Hawaii
http://www.state.hi.us/tax

Idaho
http://www2.state.id.us/tax/questions.htm#SALES%20AND%20USE
%20TAX%20(Section%20800)

Illinois
http://www.revenue.state.il.us

Indiana
http://www.ai.org/dor/taxforms/s-wforms.html

Iowa
http://www.state.ia.us/tax/taxlaw/taxtypes.html#sales

Kansas
http://www.ksrevenue.org

Kentucky
http://revenue.ky.gov/salestax_info.htm

Louisiana
http://www.rev.state.la.us/sections/business/sales.asp#sales

Maine
http://www.state.me.us/revenue/salesuse/homepage.html

Maryland
http://business.marylandtaxes.com/taxinfo/salesanduse/default.asp

Massachusetts
http://www.dor.state.ma.us/help/guides/stg_form.htm

Michigan
http://www.michigan.gov/treasury

Minnesota
http://www.taxes.state.mn.us/taxes/sales/index.shtml

Mississippi
http://www.mstc.state.ms.us/taxareas/sales/main.htm

Missouri
http://www.dor.mo.gov/tax/business/sales

Montana
http://discoveringmontana.com/revenue/css/3forbusinesses/01taxesli
censesfees/g-salestax/default.asp

Nebraska
http://www.revenue.state.ne.us/salestax.htm

Nevada
http://tax.state.nv.us

New Hampshire
http://www.state.nh.us/revenue/meals+rentals/index.htm

New Jersey
http://www.state.nj.us/treasury/taxation/index.html?hotelfee.htm
~mainFrame

New Mexico
http://www.state.nm.us/tax

New York
http://www.tax.state.ny.us/Forms/sales_cur_forms.htm

North Carolina
http://www.dor.state.nc.us/taxes/sales

North Dakota
http://www.state.nd.us/taxdpt/salesanduse

Ohio
http://tax.ohio.gov/business_taxes_sales.html

Oklahoma
http://www.oktax.state.ok.us/btforms.html

Oregon
http://www.dor.state.or.us

Pennsylvania
http://www.revenue.state.pa.us/revenue/taxonomy/taxonomy.asp?
DLN=3637

Rhode Island
http://www.tax.state.ri.us/info/synopsis/syntoc.htm

South Carolina
http://www2.sctax.org/esales

South Dakota
http://www.state.sd.us/drr2/Revenue.html

Tennessee
http://www.state.tn.us/revenue/tntaxes/salesanduse.htm

Texas
http://www.window.state.tx.us/taxinfo/sales/new_business.html

Utah
http://tax.utah.gov/sales/index.html

Vermont
http://www.state.vt.1/tax/index.htm

Virginia
http://www.tax.state.va.us/site.cfm?alias=SalesUseTax

Washington
http://dor.wa.gov/content/citizen/citizn_saleuse.asp

Washington, D.C.
http://dc.gov/index.asp

West Virginia
http://www.state.wv.us/taxdiv

Wisconsin
http://www.dor.state.wi.us/html/taxsales.html

Wyoming
http://revenue.state.wy.us/doclistout.asp?div=12&dtype=6

D

LEARNING CENTERS

This appendix provides a list of learning centers across the United States and in Canada. You can take many short courses on computer skills and Web site design through these learning centers. Look for author Christine Karpinski's "How to Purchase Vacation Properties" and "How to Rent by Owner" seminars in these locations.

Albany, NY: The Knowledge Network, http://www.knowledgenetwork.org

Albuquerque, NM: Sageways, http://www.sageways.org

Atlanta, GA: The Knowledge Shop, http://www.knowledgeshopatlanta.com

Boston, MA: Boston Learning Society, http://www.bostonlearningsociety.com

Calgary, Alberta: The Learning Annex, http://www.learningannex.com

Chicago, IL: Discovery Center, http://www.discoverycenter.com

Denver, CO: Colorado Free University, http://www.freeu.com

Edmonton, Alberta: The Learning Annex, http://www.learningannex
.com

Houston, TX: Leisure Learning Unlimited, http://www.llu.com

Los Angeles, CA: The Learning Annex, http://www.learningannex
.com

Minneapolis, MN: The Learning Annex, http://www.learningannex
.com

Monterey, CA: Center-for, http://www.center-for.com

New York, NY: The Learning Annex, http://www.learningannex.com

Newport, RI: Newport Learning Connection, http://www.newport
learningconnection.com

Orlando, FL: The Knowledge Shop, http://www.knowledgeshop
orlando.com

Philadelphia, PA: Mt. Airy Learning Tree, http://www.mtairylearning
tree.org

Providence, RI: Learning Connection–Providence, http://www.learn
connect.com

Rochester, NY: Rochester Info-Courses, http://www.infocourses.com

Sacramento, CA: Learning Exchange, http://www.learningexchange
.com

San Diego, CA: The Learning Annex, http://www.learningannex.com

San Francisco, CA: The Learning Annex, http://www.learningannex
.com

Seattle, WA: Discover U, http://www.discoveru.org

Tampa, FL: Baywinds, http://www.baywinds.net

Toronto, Ontario: The Learning Annex, http://www.learningannex
.com

Vancouver, BC: The Learning Annex, http://www.learningannex.com

Washington, DC: First Class, http://www.takeaclass.org

E

RECOMMENDED RESOURCES

Please note that the following people and companies have given the author permission to use their copyrighted information in this book. The author only includes those that she truly believes in.

Holiday Isle Properties
Jack Simpson
842 Highway 98 East
Destin, FL 32541
850-837-0092
http://www.holidayisle.net

Jack at Holiday Isle Properties offers real estate sales, full-service vacation property management, and partnership programs at 0 percent commission.

Equity Trust Company
225 Burns Road
Elyria, OH 44035
440-323-5491
http://trustetc.com

The Equity Trust Company is a leading provider of truly self-directed individual retirement accounts (IRAs) and small business retirement plans. Clients at Equity Trust have the option to invest their retirement funds in areas where they have knowledge and expertise. Equity Trust IRA investment options include real estate IRAs, mortgages/deeds of trust, and private placement IRAs.

Amy Ashcroft Greener
Copywriting, Photography, & Image Development
17366 Ida West Rd.
Petersburg, MI 49270
734-279-1140
thecreativeedge4copy@yahoo.com
http://www.swayingpines.com

Amy provides Web writing and image consulting services for vacation rental property owners. She is a contributing author to *How to Rent Vacation Properties by Owner–The Complete Guide to Buy, Manage, Furnish, Rent, Maintain and Advertise Your Vacation Rental Investment.*

EscapeHomes.com
1550 Bryant Street, Suite 525
San Francisco, CA 94103
415-252-9500
http://www.escapehomes.com

EscapeHomes.com—The Smart Source for Second Homes. This site helps people find vacation, investment, and retirement real estate. It includes homes to view, profiles of communities, and agent listings. It also features articles about owning a dream home.

Barbara McNichol
5090 N. Camino de la Cumbre
Tucson, AZ 85750
520-615-7910
editor@barbaramcnichol.com
http://www.barbaramcnichol.com

The editor of this book works with authors and publishers to provide excellent editorial services for manuscripts and marketing materials.

Broderick Perkins
San Jose, CA
info@deadlinenews.com
http://www.deadlinenews.com

Broderick Perkins is executive editor of San Jose, CA–based DeadlineNews.com, an editorial content and consulting firm. Perkins has been a consumer and real estate journalist for more than 25 years.

Rent One Online
269 Mt. Herman Rd. #205
Scotts Valley, CA 95066
831-438-3141
http://www.RentOneOnline.com

Rent One Online raises the bar for the vacation rental industry with tools that connect the vacation rental manager/owner with the traveler throughout the "vacation lifecycle." This service improves the experience for all.

Marketing & Scheduling
Gee Dunsten
408 Cobblers Green
Salisbury, MD 21801
443-523-0023
Gee@gee-dunsten.com
http://www.gee-dunsten.com

Gee Dunsten, a graduate of the University of Maryland, entered the real estate business in 1972. Starting in residential sales, he progressed to general sales manager, then owner/broker in ten years. In 1986, he sold his business and returned to his first love, selling real estate. Gee is an active sales agent, having closed more than $200 million in sales. He is a senior instructor with the Council of Residential Specialists and served as its 2001 president. Gee is also president of Gee Dunsten Seminars, Inc., a partner in Culver and Dunsten Builders, and the marketing/sales VP of Legacy Development Corporation and broker/owner of Legacy Realty, Inc. He is the coauthor of the book *Mega-Million Dollar Secrets, Power Pack 1 and 2* computer programs, and a tape series, *Blow Your Own Horn.*

With all of his career accomplishments, Gee views his greatest success as the building of his family. Gee and his wife, Susan, have five children and four grandchildren. They reside in Salisbury, Maryland.

Meredith McKenzie
Licensed California Real Estate Broker
Certified Recreation & Resort Specialist
Serving Ventura Coast & Kern River Valley, California
805-455-3955
meredith@meredithmckenzie.com

Meredith McKenzie is a licensed California real estate broker with more than ten years professional experience in the Southern California marketplace. A graduate of Loyola Law School, Meredith brings both her personal experience as a vacation home owner and her professional expertise as a Certified Recreation and Resort Specialist to her real estate practice.

David K. Drescher
Certified Insurance Counselor
Drescher Insurance
92 Main Street
Cheshire, CT 06410
203-272-2122
http://www.drescherins.com
ddrescher@drescherins.com

Drescher Insurance is a full-service insurance agency offering comprehensive property and liability coverage as well as employee benefits programs for businesses, individuals, and families.

Wallace J. Conway
HomePro Inspections
12708 San Jose Blvd.
Jacksonville, FL 32223
904-268-8211
http://www.WallyConway.com
http://www.GoHomePro.com

Speaker, Author, HomePro Inspections . . . *It's About Knowing!*

HomePro Inspections is a leading provider of home inspection and building consultation services. HomePro President Wally Conway is a frequent contributor to radio, television, and print media on matters related to home inspections.

Shannyn Stevenson ABR®
Realtor and Accredited Buyer's Representative
Destin to the Beaches of South Walton
850-259-1874
Toll-free: 800-596-7006
Shannyn@KnowDestin.com
http://www.KnowDestin.com

Shannyn is a full-time real estate professional who offers years of experience buying and selling homes in the Destin and Santa Rosa Beach markets in Florida.

Christine Hrib Karpinski's first and most important job is being a stay-at-home mom. She fell into self-managing vacation properties when she couldn't afford to hire a management company to rent out her Florida condo. Not only did she learn to successfully "rent by owner" but realized others wanted to know how to do it, too.

She started sharing her knowledge through a column in *Gulf Coast Condo Owner Magazine*. The rest, as they say, is history. Christine and her book, *How to Rent Vacation Properties by Owner: The Complete Guide to Buy, Manage, Furnish, Rent, Maintain and Advertise Your Vacation Rental Investment,* have been featured on bankrate.com, CNNfn, CBS Marketwatch Radio, *Good Day Sacramento,* MSNBC TV, and in *Realty Times,* the *San Francisco Chronicle,* the *Chicago Tribune,* the *Calgary Herald,* and many others.

When she's not teaching or taking care of her family, you'll find Christine creating pottery in a studio, singing in her church choir, or relaxing on the beach in Destin, Florida. She lives with her husband, Tom; son, Zachary; and two Nova Scotia Duck Tollers, Trumpet and Piccolo.

Share the message!

Bulk discounts
Discounts start at only 10 copies and range from 30% to 55% off retail price based on quantity.

Custom publishing
Private label a cover with your organization's name and logo. Or, tailor information to your needs with a custom pamphlet that highlights specific chapters.

Ancillaries
Workshop outlines, videos, and other products are available on select titles.

Dynamic speakers
Engaging authors are available to share their expertise and insight at your event.

**Call Dearborn Trade Special Sales at
1-800-621-9621, ext. 4444,
or e-mail trade@dearborn.com**

Dearborn™
Trade Publishing

A **Kaplan Professional** Company